Sober Mama

Breaking Free from the Bottle
A Woman's Journey to Sobriety and
Practical Tips for Quitting

RACHAEL SHEPHARD

SOBER MAMA

An Hachette UK Company
www.hachette.co.uk

Vie Books, an imprint of Summersdale Publishers
Part of Octopus Publishing Group Limited
Carmelite House
50 Victoria Embankment
LONDON
EC4Y 0DZ
UK

www.summersdale.com

The authorized representative in the EEA is Hachette Ireland,
8 Castlecourt Centre, Castleknock Road, Castleknock,
Dublin 15, D15 YF6A, Ireland

Printed and bound by Clays Ltd, Suffolk, NR35 1ED

ISBN: 978-1-83799-433-5

This FSC® label means that materials used for the product have been responsibly sourced

MIX
Paper | Supporting
responsible forestry
FSC® C104740

Substantial discounts on bulk quantities of Summersdale books are available to corporations, professional associations and other organizations. For details contact general enquiries: telephone: +44 (0) 1243 771107 or email: enquiries@summersdale.com.

For Arthur and Alfie.
I love you both infinity times infinity.

Contents

Introduction – Why I Quit Alcohol for Good

> "The greatest glory in living lies not in never falling, but in rising every time we fall."

Attributed to Oliver Goldsmith

Once upon a time, I was the quintessential drunken lush, known mainly for my tendency to indulge in heavy drinking and late-night escapades. The friend who first comes to mind when you want a big night out. The one who always takes things a bit too far and ends up regretting it in the morning – the embodiment of fun, chaos and frequent public embarrassment. Now, I'm a sober introvert, and I'm very happy to be. But more about the "new me" later.

For well over two decades, I was a devoted drunken reveller. When I had children, I slowed down a little and took a break from my boozy antics. But as the baby years passed and the school runs began, I jumped back into the party scene like it was 1999. Well, almost. My idea of "partying" changed a tad. Instead of hitting the bar and knocking back shots of tequila, you could find me leaning against my kitchen counter with a bottle of Pinot Grigio in hand. In my pyjamas. At five in the afternoon. I became a master of "mum partying". Kate Moss used to be my inspiration as a party-mad single woman (before she got sober). When I became a mum of two boys and subsequently got divorced, Sarah Turner, the delightful author of *The Unmumsy Mum*, took Kate's place as my role model of choice. I found her words soothing while trying to navigate the mammoth task of motherhood, juggling a full-time job and a rapidly deteriorating social life. She was a woman who was prepared to write the unadulterated truth about motherhood down on paper, namely how shit of a job I thought it was, and unlike the perfect Facebook mum tribe, she also referred to her children as little "arseholes". Another inspirational figure to me was Gill Sims, the author of *Why Mummy Drinks*. She recognized that wine is the only solution to pretty much everything – especially mothering – and these were words that I very much needed to hear in the early years of parenthood.

I have a full-time job working 40 hours a week in law enforcement, I run a small business as a side hustle (who doesn't need extra money – have you seen the price of petrol and cooking oil!) and I'm a single mother of two boys: Arthur and Alfie. Before I gave up drinking, I believed that I had my ducks in a row. I used to pride myself on being a weekend warrior – juggling countless activities with my kids, whipping up gourmet meals from scratch and still finding time to run three miles a day and go out with my friends. I thought I was killing it.

I considered myself to be a multitasking queen. However, I used to polish off up to two bottles of wine each night and felt like I was wading through treacle every day. I was the epitome of a "high-functioning alcoholic". I wasn't smashing life – I was simply crashing through it, while simultaneously getting shit done. High-functioning maybe, but a total fucking mess.

I didn't recognize that I had a problem with alcohol for a long time, largely because I was still able to get up each day and tear through a to-do list like Superwoman on cocaine. I wore the ability to drink wine like it was going out of fashion, as a badge of honour and something to be proud of. I would regularly announce to my fellow drinking mummies at the school gate, "I smashed a bottle of wine by myself last night. I'm so hungover!" The response was always one of commendation: "Well done! Good skills!"

On the surface, I would enthusiastically rave about wine and laugh off the hangover. I wanted people to see me as the "fun and crazy" mum. I made jokes about drinking because there was a dark side to my life that I tried really hard to minimize, masking it with humour. It was easier to pretend. I didn't want to face the truth. I couldn't face it. I suffered from crippling anxiety for all of the 25 years that I drank. Ten out of ten, 24/7, overwhelming anxiety that I could only abate by drinking wine. I would count down the hours each day until it was time to open a bottle. Any time after five in the evening was acceptable – it says so on those "it's five o'clock somewhere" signs. Most days, it was mental torture waiting for the moment I could grab a glass and release my body from the stress, tension and madness of each day. I hankered for those first few sips. It was like flipping a switch in my body, going from stress mode to relaxation central, melting away the crippling mental anguish and numbing the physical tightening in my chest. Instant relief. I needed that. Life was just too hard without some chemical help to take the edge off.

The problem was that the relief only lasted for a few short hours. I woke up at three in the morning, like clockwork, with a huge jolt of fear. I would mentally trace back through the evening.

I had wine. A lot of wine. I don't remember going to bed. What day is it? Ah, it's Tuesday. I didn't go out – so I couldn't have done anything bad. It's a school night. Phew!

Then I would tell myself to go back to sleep because there wasn't anything to fear. Sometimes it worked. Other times I would toss and turn uncomfortably until my alarm went off.

Then there were those nights. If you drink a lot, then you will know the ones I'm talking about. The nights where I would wake up in the early hours with a surge of overwhelming panic – like I'd been shot.

What day is it? Saturday? Where am I? How did I get home? Where did I end up last night? Did I upset anyone? Who did I message?

Then came the health worries.

How long can I keep drinking like this before my body gives up? I might have liver cirrhosis already. I really need to cut down. I have to learn to moderate. But I know I can't do that! I'm going to end up seriously ill. How can I do this to my children? I'll leave them motherless if I die!

Self-loathing, fear, guilt and anxiety – over and over – this is the cycle I lived in. Until around four in the afternoon when the panic and self-loathing began to wear off and that itch for wine started to irritate under my skin. The creeping feeling of emptiness, like hunger. I'd walk through the door following the school run, having slogged out a day at work while feeling like utter shit. My boys would inevitably be fighting in the hallway before I'd even got through the front door.

Fuck this. I need wine. I need wine like I need air. No one can parent in this day and age without drinking. If I die, I die. Who fucking cares! Pinot will fix that. One glass, and I won't care about anything. Everyone does it. Ninety per cent of adults drink. I'm NORMAL!

The sad thing is that last statement is true. I was normal. I don't believe in defining myself by the dreaded "A" word and announcing myself as an alcoholic, but in the spirit of introduction – my name is Rachael, and I had a major problem with alcohol. And so, I think, do many people. I don't believe any of us are to blame, which is why I don't like the stigma of the "A" word. We live in a society where drinking is socially acceptable, endorsed and – worse than that – expected. The reality is that we regularly consume one of the most addictive and damaging drugs known to humankind – of course we are all bloody hooked!

Drinking is an integral part of our culture, particularly in the UK. We are constantly surrounded by positive images of alcohol. We give each other cards on birthdays, joking about alcohol consumption. We celebrate and commiserate everything by popping a cork. However, the reality is that we are ingesting poison – ethanol – the same substance used to sterilize medical equipment. Do you remember when Donald Trump suggested injecting disinfectant as a means to combat Covid? We all laughed at his utter stupidity. But the truth is, we are doing the same thing by drinking booze. It's just ethanol, a toxic sanitizer and the same base drug found in every alcoholic drink. Here's a fun fact: just 80 to 90 millilitres of pure ethanol can kill you. Take a moment to think about that. Alcohol is a drug that is so noxious that even in tiny quantities it will cause your demise. We water it down, package it in pretty bottles, mix it with sweeteners, kill ourselves slowly and tell ourselves it's a treat – we deserve it. How crazy is that?

How have we, as a society, collectively opened our eyes to the dangers of smoking, yet still treat alcohol like a friend? We laugh about hangovers, accuse anyone who doesn't drink of being boring and suggest alcohol as a solution to pretty much everything. Yet, booze is the single biggest killer of working-age adults, and, scarily, it's legal in most countries.

There are no benefits to drinking (I know this is hard to believe, but bear with me) and all of the myths we believe to be positive are simply not true. My favourite myth is "red wine is good for the heart". I held onto statements like this – much like someone drowning would cling to a life raft. It was so easy to dismiss the risks of consuming alcohol when science-based articles suggest it might be healthy! I read one article which suggested that red wine lowers heart disease. It can thin the blood, which may reduce heart disease for a time – but it also causes high blood pressure, heart failure, heart attack, irregular heart rhythms and strokes. Ethanol attacks every single organ in the human body. So drinking for any perceived benefit is a little like someone telling you to let go of a life raft – because the benefit of drowning is that you can have a nice little swim first. In this book, I am going to dismantle some more of these myths and throw in some very amusing drunken stories for good measure – because, let's be honest, no great story started with a fruit juice, right? Mmm. We'll see.

I decided to quit drinking for good in November 2021 – to be exact, on the eighteenth of November. My decision to give up booze for good came at the end of a tumultuous couple of years. I very suddenly and unexpectedly lost my darling mum right at the beginning of the Covid pandemic, while I was in the middle of a home extension and had to move in with my then in-laws. I left my husband and went through an acrimonious divorce – all while working full-time, running a small business, raising two young boys alone, suffering from a debilitating health condition (ulcerative colitis) and supporting my poor, bereft dad who had lost my mum after 42 years together. It was a bloody rough time in my life and I coped, as one would fully expect, by numbing myself with copious amounts of wine on a nightly basis.

At the point I quit drinking, I went from consuming between one to two bottles of wine a night to absolutely nothing. I'm completely sober, and I have never felt better. I'm still in disbelief. I never envisaged that I would be able to give up wine. I didn't think it was a remote possibility for someone like me.

I've experienced countless benefits since quitting booze. A bottle of wine contains a whopping 600 calories, give or take. I was consuming up to two bottles a night at the time I decided to give up. A saving of 1,200 calories a day! The "anxiety" I suffered for almost 25 years disappeared almost entirely. Depression, much improved. Random pains in my stomach, gone. Bank balance, much healthier! There are so many more benefits I can't wait to share, but the biggest one of all: I am now a mummy who is present.

I thought I was a great mum. Granted, I did some fabulous things with my children, and I have always showered them with affection and love, but a great mum? It's only now I look back and think, Thank God I quit while they're young. Hopefully, my kids will have no memory of who I was when I was drinking. I'm ashamed of who I became: a mum who put her kids to bed early so she could drink herself into a nightly coma. I was irritable all the time and quick to anger. I knew for a long time that I needed to quit, but I was so worried about becoming boring and not being able to enjoy life or cope without alcohol that I continued to drink and tell myself I was just the same as everyone else. I wasn't that bad.

It wasn't too long ago that I loved to smoke. It was cool to smoke! Smoking was widely accepted as being fashionable for many years – so accepted that you could even smoke on a plane, in restaurants, shops and at the cinema. It's only now that we see smoking for the vile and disgusting habit it is.

Did it suddenly become disgusting and abhorrent? No! It was always so. The only thing that changed was our perception. As a society, we collectively opened our eyes to the truth. Smoking became unacceptable. Decidedly uncool. The world over, our pack mentality shifted and did a 180-degree flip. I think alcohol will go the same way.

We currently view alcohol as a socially accepted, deserved, well-loved treat. We work hard. Life is tough. We earn the right to relax. Of course we do. But here's the thing – alcohol doesn't actually help us to relax. It's a drug. We feel the effects of the ethanol soothe and numb our pain and worries. When it wears off, we get withdrawal symptoms – which incidentally are exactly the same as anxiety. Alcohol doesn't help you to relax. It's a lie. Alcohol merely stops the symptoms of withdrawal and temporarily blocks out the negative mental chatter.

Alcohol had been my crutch for so long. I had to learn how to deal with even the most basic of emotions instead of relying on chemical help. As it turns out, I wasn't much more emotionally intelligent than my children! I spent my days trying to teach them how to deal with playground disputes, how to share and how to cope with failure, but my own way of dealing with all emotions was to head to the fridge and grab the Pinot. I was so scared of life that I spent half of it totally numb and the other half feeling like crap, counting down the hours until I could anaesthetize myself. Looking at it like that, I just think, Wow. This is so sad. I was going to live a whole life and miss it because I wasn't actually present.

Every positive feeling we derive from alcohol is actually just a debt that we incur. We borrow tomorrow's happiness – it is not given to us for free. Alcohol provides temporary enjoyment, but there is always a trade-off. When we have one glass of wine, alcohol takes the edge off life and offers a little perceived relaxation. Ideally, we would like to stop at one, but alcohol is sneaky and highly addictive. For those of us that struggle to stop at one glass, we often crave a second, knowing it will take more from us, but our inhibitions are already lowered, and it's so much easier to say "fuck it" and have another drink. With each additional glass, the trade-off becomes more significant. At best, we will have a dreadful hangover; at worst, we risk having blackouts; having no memory of being rude or abusive; becoming easy victims of sexual assault and violence; engaging in drink driving; having suicidal tendencies; and losing homes, families and loved ones. The risks only increase the more we drink.

We tend to view alcoholics as those who have lost everything to booze. But alcoholism doesn't discriminate. The homeless person sat in a doorway drinking Special Brew and the banker sipping Dom Perignon in a beautiful London bar are taking exactly the same drug – ethanol. It's nothing short of insanity that someone who drinks copious amounts of excruciatingly expensive wine is labelled a connoisseur, and yet someone who drinks a lot of cheap booze is the social definition of an alcoholic. The only actual difference between these people is income and a postcode.

Having money can actually be a catalyst for an addiction problem – significant income increases the accessibility of drink and drugs. The National Institute for Occupational Safety and Health compiles an annual list of jobs with the highest suicide rates. Shockingly, at the top of the list are some of the most highly paid (and stressful) careers. According to the website Mental Health Daily, "Year after year, both dentist and doctor remain among the occupations with the highest suicide rates… requiring significant levels of aptitude, sacrifice and education seem to be those with above-average risk of suicide." Doctors in particular are well known for being prone to developing alcohol and drug addictions. This is often attributed to their demanding work environment, knowledge of, and access to, medication, and stress-related mental illness.

You might think you're lucky to have a great, lucrative profession, where drinking nightly is not only common but also encouraged, as it's essential to entertaining clients. But what's the trade-off? Who knows? Liver cirrhosis at 45, losing your driving licence, stroke at 50, heart attack or suicide. Does that sound extreme? The truth is that if you drink any alcohol at all, you are at risk of addiction and mental health decline. Depression and anxiety are an epidemic the world over – but I often wonder what would happen if doctors prescribed 90 days of sobriety to every person who presented with poor mental health? How many people would discover that they're okay and alcohol is responsible for most of their massive lows? I've been there. Alcohol has taken me to the absolute depths of despair. Sobriety has been the most peaceful, anxiety-free period of time I've had since I was a child.

I'm hoping that you will read this book and begin to question your beliefs about alcohol. As I explain my journey to sobriety, I hope you can reflect on your own life, and maybe this will resonate with you and help you make small positive changes. If just one person reads this and thinks, I'm going to have a break from alcohol, I'll be pretty chuffed. Any time away from the sauce is beneficial, and who knows, you might decide to try sobriety for good once you read about the extraordinary pleasure that comes with being free from booze. I really hope I don't come across as preachy. This certainly isn't my intention. I have the utmost respect for anyone who is struggling with addiction – you need the most incredible resilience to battle through each day in pain – and I have zero judgement. I've been there, and I know just how terrible it is to be in that cycle. I've just discovered the most incredible joy in becoming sober, and I'm excited to share the benefits with you. Most of all, I want to dismantle the theory that being sober is tedious and no fun.

If you are currently drinking and desperate to find a way out, it may be tempting to skip straight to the How to Quit chapter, but please don't do this. It's important to read the chapters before it. I believe that unravelling the myths about alcohol is the first step to quitting and serves as a solid foundation for getting sober. The great news is that once you've dismantled the myths about alcohol, you've cracked the hardest part of quitting. It's a little like riding a bike: once learned, it can't be unlearned. This is no different. Once you discover the truth about alcohol, you crack the hardest piece of the puzzle, and you'll never view it in the same way again.

I'm not going to lie; the idea of spending the rest of my life without wine scared the shit out of me. I was terrified that people would think I was no longer fun. Being fun is who I am, and I was scared of losing friendships by becoming the "boring, sober one". The only time I took a decent break from alcohol was during my two pregnancies (and, even then, not completely). Alcohol was a daily part of my life and I felt like I was starting over. I literally felt like I had to learn how to live again because, like so many people, when I feel any emotion other than happiness, I want to squash it immediately. I had to learn to be sober like I learned to play the guitar; it's a skill that requires work and practice. But if I can be a heavy drinker for 25 years and then quit for good, anyone can, including you, and I'm going to show you how.

Moderate, or Quit for Good?

> "Moderation is a fatal thing. Nothing succeeds like excess."
>
> Oscar Wilde

I spent many hours trying to work out why I couldn't manage one glass at a time, when so many others can do so with relative ease. I knew deep down, for a long time, that one day I would have to quit for good. If I wanted to live a long life and be healthy, I had no choice but to stop completely. I tried to moderate enough times over the years to know that this just wasn't an option for me; it was always elusive. Whether or not to moderate seems to be a question many people ask themselves when they examine their relationship with alcohol. So, what should you do? Could you moderate if it came to it? Could you be one of those people who many problem drinkers aspire to be? My belief is that if you can moderate, you're always at risk of entering the danger zone. If you're like me and can't stop at one glass, you're actually very lucky. The universe has done you a favour. Why? Because alcohol is absolutely the one substance you really want to think about in "all-or-nothing" terms. I no longer aspire to be someone who has the ability to moderate their use of the planet's most addictive, destructive poison.

Let's think for a minute about why people drink. Alcohol is designed to create a feeling, a sensation in your body. You probably don't drink it for the taste. You certainly do not use it to hydrate; it does quite the opposite. In its pure form, ethanol tastes absolutely disgusting. Why? Because Mother Nature very cleverly equipped your tongue with tastebuds – so you have the ability to assess what you ingest, to make sure it's safe. Think caveman days. Your body has a fantastically clever inbuilt "poison detector" system. If your tastebuds like what you're consuming, it's most likely harmless. If it tastes horrendous, it's probably going to do you some damage. The producers of all types of alcohol have very cleverly masked the horrendous taste of ethanol by mixing it with some other beverage, juice or syrup to make it more palatable. Does it taste great? Really think about this. Does the addition of ethanol make it taste better than a non-alcoholic drink? It *can't*. Because ethanol tastes absolutely vile. We tolerate the taste because we like the effect, or we like whatever lovely flavour it's been masked with. The weaker the alcoholic drink, the better the taste, generally. Then we get to the likes of stronger alcohol, like tequila – now do you think that's a delightful, refreshing, tasty drink to quench your thirst on a hot summer's day? I highly doubt it, judging by the fact it's served in a shot glass so you can neck it as quickly as possible – and with salt and lime so you can quickly neutralize the flavour – all while trying not to vomit.

I think we can safely establish that very few people drink alcohol solely for the taste. So why do moderators have just one glass? For the exact same reason that other people have ten: to feel better, to take the edge off and lessen the impact of life. They may be able to stop at one, but make no mistake, moderators use alcohol to ease the pain – the same as heavy drinkers. They just happen to have an "off switch", or simply less pain to kill – for now. If you're in early sobriety, have given up drinking completely, or have previously had a stint off the sauce, you will have inevitably encountered a conversation with a moderator. Have you ever noticed that every single person who moderates their alcohol consumption will respond to you in exactly the same way? Tell a moderator that you don't drink, and they'll explain why they do. Why is that? Because they are addicted to some degree, and they know it's harmful. They want to feel better and justify their own consumption. When I go to a bar and someone offers me an alcoholic drink, I politely decline and give one of many reasons why I don't consume alcohol. My latest response to strangers is, "Because if I drink alcohol, I'll get my beer goggles on, suddenly everyone looks attractive, and I'll be sucking your dick later... and I really don't want to do that." Just joking.

Normally, I say that I've quit because I have a bad relationship with alcohol, and then I wait for the inevitable reply: their justification. Moderators will tell you in 20 different ways why they drink alcohol or why it's not an issue. Don't believe me? Test it. The next time you politely decline a drink in a bar, wait for the reply. I find it usually goes something like this: "Ah, you see, I have always been able to stop after one or two. I'm lucky." "Oh, that's such a shame for you! I've never had a problem with alcohol. I can take it or leave it." "Oh, I feel bad for you! I don't drink during the week at all. I just drink on weekends." "I don't need to drink. I just like to every now and then socially." This isn't a criticism of people who choose to drink, just an observation – when I was drinking, I used to respond in exactly the same way.

There are thousands of variations, but the sentiment is clear: drinkers feel the need to justify to themselves and to others that they are different. They could never be an addict. They would never be the person reaching for a glass in the morning. They're immune. They don't have a problem. Alcohol is an addictive substance. If you drink frequently enough, it will become a dependency. Human beings cannot protect themselves from this. Drink enough, and eventually, you'll become physically reliant, moderator or not. Remember, moderators drink for the same reasons as full-blown alcoholics – to take the edge off their negative emotions.

This might seem like a bold statement, but it's important to think about it. If you don't need to drink, why would you choose to do it, knowing that it can lead to the most horrendous problems? When someone says they "like to drink socially", what do they actually mean? They mean that, at social occasions, everyone else will be drinking, and they don't want to feel left out. They mean that drinking will lower their inhibitions and make it easier to talk to people they don't know. They mean that social occasions can cause anxiety, so they need to induce relaxation. Moderators may be able to moderate, but they are on the same path as every other person who drinks alcohol. They're using ethanol to change their emotional state.

So what? What does it matter if someone can moderate, and they enjoy it? Why shouldn't we want to be like them? Isn't that the ideal place to be? Firstly, moderators are not free. They're a slave to alcohol, the same as a problem drinker, just not as far along the sliding scale of addiction. Secondly, and most importantly, if you use alcohol to numb your feelings, to feel better in the moment, or to soften the impact of life, you run a massive risk of rapidly spiralling out of control if you suffer a major life event or trauma. Why? Because if you use alcohol to quash the feeling of being mildly uncomfortable, you're more than likely going to use alcohol to knock out feelings of despair or heartbreak. If your coping mechanism for a stressful day is just one glass of wine, how will you react when there is a major stressful event? More wine. Much more wine.

Moderation keeps the monster alive. If you find yourself wishing you could just stop at one glass, remind yourself that black-and-white thinking will save you. You're not weaker because you can't moderate, you're stronger, because when you're sober and the shit hits the fan, you will deal with your emotions by learning to cope with life and facing your fears head-on.

One of Many Drunken Stories

> "Rock bottom became the solid foundation
> on which I rebuilt my life."

J. K. Rowling

Many years ago, before I had children, I lived in the Cayman Islands, specifically Grand Cayman, a picture-perfect island, stunningly beautiful, with miles and miles of glorious white sand and gorgeous blue ocean. As the island only spans 26 miles, there is very little to do. However, if you're into water sports, there are countless activities. I wasn't, but there were two things the island had in abundance that I loved: restaurants and bars. I spent a few years hopping from one bar to another, and instead of enjoying the glorious beaches, I would regularly spend my days recovering from hangovers in my air-conditioned apartment.

There were various festivals routinely celebrated on the island. My first one was Mardi Gras, and I was invited to go to a beach bar with a group of new friends I had met at work. The bar was called Kaibo, and it was situated right on the beach, with a veranda where various people were throwing handfuls of bead necklaces to the crowd below. I'm told that it's a tradition for beads to be thrown towards women who flash their boobs, but luckily for me, this was not an endorsed practice in Cayman. I wouldn't have flashed my boobs when I was sober. However, when drunk, this would have seemed like a most excellent idea, and I would certainly have partaken in said activity. Probably not the best first impression to give to my new friends.

When I arrived at the bar, I went straight to one of the drink stands that had been set up especially for the festival. I opted for some sort of punch, which was rum-based and strong. This was a disaster waiting to happen. Wine had always been my tipple of choice. One of the reasons for this is that I had some degree of control over how drunk I got. I could feel when I was getting hammered, and more often than not, I was at least able to stop before I got to the vomiting stage. I spent my teenage years slamming shots and have spent more nights hugging a toilet than I dare to think about. With age and experience, I believed myself to be far wiser, and wine seemed to be the answer to at least limiting the level of destruction of a heavy session. Of course, there were still many nights where I overdid this too – but I told myself that not drinking spirits meant that I was grown-up and actually pretty sensible. So, why did I opt for rum when I knew that drinking spirits was likely to have disastrous results? Because the queue for the main bar was long, and I didn't want to wait to get a drink. Immediate alcohol consumption, however calamitous the consequences, was preferable to waiting for ten minutes.

After just one drink, I felt tipsy. I have no idea how much rum there was in my first glass, but it's fair to say it was a significant measure, and I had no intention of stopping. I also hadn't eaten, which was cardinal drinking sin number one. I couldn't tell you how many drinks I had, but I was frightfully paralytic. I spent the day throwing myself around the dance floor – which had the benefit of being on the beach, so I didn't hurt myself during the many times I fell over on the sand. Ideal! I recall suddenly and desperately needing the bathroom and there being a queue so long that I knew I wouldn't be able to hold it. One of the few memories I have of that day was squatting behind an open car door and peeing in the street – oh, so attractive.

Someone drove me back to my apartment. It could have been a friend, or a total stranger – I didn't care. I was just glad to be home. My last memory of the night is crashing around the kitchen looking for a pair of scissors. I'd decided to cut off the wristband that I'd been given when I first arrived at the bar, to prove that I'd paid for entry. But I couldn't find any scissors. I'd only recently moved into the apartment, and it was fully furnished. I had no clue if there even were any scissors – so I opted for a sharp knife instead. I put the blade under the wristband and, in one very clumsy, drunken move, I pulled hard to cut through the plastic. The band was thinner than I'd realized, and the force I'd applied was overzealous. I sliced through the wristband and smacked myself in the face. I didn't feel any pain. I was too hammered. I just saw the blood – a lot of blood. I stumbled to the bathroom and stuck a towel on my face to stem the bleeding. I have a vague recollection of applying some plasters to my face before I crawled up the stairs and into bed. Within seconds, I was catatonic.

When I woke up the next morning, I had a throbbing headache, felt violently sick, and could feel dried blood on my face. My sheets looked like a crime scene. Worriedly, I ventured towards the bathroom to assess the damage. As I peeled off the plasters, I was horrified to find that I had gouged out a chunk of flesh near my eyebrow, and had a large cut across my eye. Worst of all, I had caused a large open slice across my cheek that was about an inch long. I knew instantly that this would scar, a permanent reminder of my stupidity. I vowed at that moment never to drink again. My face did scar, but luckily it has lessened over time and is easily coverable with make-up. Nonetheless, it serves as a daily reminder of the consequences of heavy drinking.

I'd like to say that this event kick-started my sobriety, or at least a period of abstinence, but two days later, I was out again, drinking wine of course. That was the solution. Once my hangover had worn off, I convinced myself that the only reason I had ended up in such a mess was that I had been drinking rum punch. I just needed to stick to wine, and then I'd be sensible.

This is the internal chatter that I continued to tell myself for many years – complete bullshit, of course. There was always an excuse or an easily concocted rationale for a drunken episode gone wrong. I hadn't stuck to wine, I hadn't eaten beforehand, I'd exercised too close to drinking – anything to explain away my behaviour. The truth is that I would excuse anything so I could carry on drinking because, to me, the only thing worse than doing something utterly stupid, was not drinking at all.

One of the biggest benefits of my sobriety is that I will never make a complete fool of myself again or do anything inherently dangerous. Yes, I'll still make mistakes and say or do things I find embarrassing, but my sober actions will not result in anything catastrophic. I can trust my own judgement. I don't panic before a night out or cringe when I look at my phone in the morning as I assess the damage of messages I've sent in a stupor. When I drank, I was constantly afraid of the damage I might cause to my life. I lived in abject fear of myself.

Am I an Alcoholic?

Pablo Picasso

Am I an alcoholic? If you've picked up this book, I'm hazarding a guess that you've asked yourself this question many times. I certainly did. I couldn't find the answer in books, blogs, podcasts or the oracle – also known as Google. Even my doctor couldn't make that diagnosis. Why? Because alcoholism isn't measurable. There is no test to determine if you're an alcoholic. There is no quantifiable definition.

In the Oxford English Dictionary, an alcoholic is defined as "a person who regularly drinks too much alcohol and cannot easily stop drinking, so that it has become an illness." So, if you cannot stop drinking, how do you know if you're addicted? Is addiction categorized by the amount you drink, or the frequency? If you have two glasses of wine, but drink every single day, is that enough for you to be labelled an alcoholic? If you only drink on a Friday and Saturday but consume four bottles of wine in a binge each week, is that indicative of an alcohol problem? Does alcoholism start when you begin drinking in the morning? Or is it simply if you drink anything at all? The World Health Organization recently published a statement in *The Lancet Public Health* explaining that when it comes to alcohol consumption, there is no safe amount that does not affect health. But addiction? Where is that benchmark?

When I gave up drinking for good, I was consuming up to two bottles of wine six nights a week. I took one day off a week to prove to myself that I wasn't physically dependent. If I could go a day without alcohol and not get the shakes, that had to be proof that I still had control. Mental dependency is quite simply getting cravings for alcohol. Physical dependency is when it becomes dangerous to abstain. In fact, it's safer to continue drinking and you should only stop with medical assistance. Why? Because physical dependency results in ethanol withdrawal. Minor ethanol withdrawal can result in tremors, anxiety and nausea. Severe alcohol withdrawal is commonly referred to as DTs (delirium tremens), which have a high mortality rate. Giving up alcohol suddenly when you're physically dependent can, therefore, quickly result in death from respiratory failure and cardiac arrhythmias.

I was able to work a full-time job, raise two young children alone and run a side-hustle business – I wasn't just coping, I was excelling. Real alcoholics, I reasoned, were surely the ones who need to drink in the mornings, the people who lose their jobs, get caught drink-driving, and ruin their close relationships before they eventually turn yellow and die from liver cirrhosis. I wasn't even close to being that bad. I was super functional. So, could I have been a functional alcoholic? According to Wikipedia, a high-functioning alcoholic is "a person who maintains jobs and relationships while exhibiting alcoholism" – except the criteria to be an alcoholic isn't clear, so I'm still none the wiser.

I've read more "quit lit" than anyone else I know, but I still can't tell you the definition of an alcoholic. I've got no quiz, mechanism or method to advise if you're one either. I do, however, have an answer for the question, "Am I an alcoholic?" So, beautiful readers, here it is: am I an alcoholic? And are you an alcoholic, for that matter?

The answer: it doesn't matter. Alcohol is toxic for everyone. Whether you're drinking vodka for breakfast, whether you're like I was – a mum drinking Pinot the second you finish the school run – whether you're sober all week and then smashing 12 cocktails on a Friday night, or you can easily moderate, anyone would benefit hugely from quitting, because nothing good comes from drinking poison in any measure, and there are zero benefits to consuming ethanol. Whether you're physically dependent, mentally dependent or barely bothered, you wouldn't mix arsenic with fruit juice and call it a treat, even if it did make you feel good for a while. If you drink enough alcohol, it makes you vomit. Why? Your body is extremely intelligent, and when it's being poisoned, it makes you throw up to try to expel the substance causing damage.

I'm not denying that I've had many fun nights while drinking, but the alcohol wasn't the cause of the fun – it was the people.

Whatever buzz or benefit you think you're getting in the short term is far outweighed by the negative consequences. Here is my list of pros and cons of drinking alcohol.

Pros:

1. *The initial feeling of relaxation, from the first sip to about 20 to 40 minutes later.*

Cons:

1. *Waking up every night at three in the morning with a surge of anxiety, lying awake tossing and turning, going over all the horrible things you've ever said and done until you get up. Self-loathing and acknowledging that you need to quit (until that evening when the craving kicks in again).*
2. *Never sleeping through the night, getting up umpteen times to go to the bathroom, gulp water or take paracetamol for the impending headache. Waking up feeling hungover, tired and grouchy.*
3. *Anyone who drinks alcohol smells terrible to sober people. I don't want my children to grow up with a memory of a mum who smelt of alcohol when they were kissed goodnight.*
4. *It's really expensive. I worked out that over the past 25 years, I've spent £100,000 on alcohol. A mind-boggling figure. Think of what you could do with such a significant pay increase!*
5. *Drinking too much makes you vomit.*

6. *Sober is sexy; drunk is the opposite. It's highly unattractive. Drunk people sound stupid too.*

7. *Drinking makes your skin look sallow, causes premature ageing, weight gain, acne and weakens your hair and nails. Attractive, hey?!*

8. *Drinking actually shrinks the size of your brain.*

9. *Alcohol causes multiple types of cancer and liver cirrhosis. It kills more people than any other drug known to humankind – and yet this is the legal one.*

10. *Alcohol lowers inhibitions. We believe it increases confidence, but Mother Nature created inhibitions for a reason – to protect us. When we drink, we make poor choices and embarrass ourselves.*

11. *Missing several hours of your life each day in "blackout". I regularly drank from around four in the afternoon. I never remembered anything past about seven each night. So much time is wasted and ultimately lost by drinking.*

12. *You never find out what you truly love or enjoy because you're numbing out the good emotions as well as the bad.*

13. *Children suffer when parents drink. Whether it's full-blown neglect or simply choosing not to play with them instead of having a drink, they suffer.*

14. *You lose countless days of your life spent recovering from heavy drinking sessions.*

15. *Alcohol causes depression.*

16. *Alcohol significantly increases domestic violence in seriousness and frequency.*

17. *Alcohol causes injuries from falling or making dangerous decisions.*
18. *Alcohol causes daily anxiety (withdrawal) that we treat by drinking more alcohol!*
19. *Alcohol destroys relationships.*
20. *You never learn to be an adult! You spend your life numbing every emotion, so you never learn to process difficult things. You live in fear. When you get scared, you stick your head in the sand and have a drink instead of maturely processing and dealing with your problems. Alcohol makes all problems worse.*

This list is by no means exhaustive. The point is that the benefits of feeling the initial alcohol fuzzy glow are far outweighed by the negative consequences. What I can say with absolute certainty is that when you quit, everything will get better. My life has changed so much more than I expected, and every day I'm surprised by new improvements and positive transformations that have come from being sober. Life is simply much better without alcohol, and my only regret is not quitting sooner – or starting in the first place, for that matter!

No one dying of liver cirrhosis ever thought they would get to that stage until it was too late. We all like to think we'd be able to stop if it really came to it, don't we? That we'll catch it just in time. Every person who has died from alcohol-related illness started by drinking the same way you and I did. No one is immune – we can all end up the one drinking in the morning. We're all on the same scale of addiction – some of us just slip further or faster along than others. Where "alcoholic" is on that gauge just doesn't matter. "Enjoying" the odd glass of poison within the recommended government allowance is still a pointless and harmful pastime. You're still somewhere on that decline – one really bad day, trauma or significant personal disaster away from increasing your intake and sliding down very, very quickly. No good can come from it.

So, do you think you're an alcoholic? Does it matter? I don't think so. But if you're asking yourself that question, then quitting for good might just be the answer you're looking for.

Speaking Sober

"Always do sober what you said you'd do when you were drunk. That will teach you to keep your mouth shut!"

Ernest Hemingway

One morning I was walking to the shop with Arthur and Alfie when I realized something incredible – I can speak *Minecraft*! Just in case you have been living under a rock, *Minecraft* is a game that involves creating various worlds, where players find their own supplies, food and create buildings and weapons to fight creatures like zombies. I do try hard to keep my kids off their tablets as much as possible, but as games go, this is a pretty cool one, because it involves a lot of creative thinking and problem-solving. Just as well, because both of my boys are obsessed with it.

Arthur and Alfie were walking a few paces in front of me, discussing *Minecraft* tactics with total seriousness: "Arthur, when we get back, we need to go into creative and build a bunker and get more armour before we hit survival, or we won't be able to beat the Ender Dragon. There were so many Creepers in the last game! I couldn't believe it. You can't even dig to get away in survival because you'll hit Bedrock."

Code:

Armour – Same meaning as in the English dictionary.

Ender Dragon – The boss bad guy; always appears in the End (dimension).

The End (dimension) – Final battle of the game against the Ender Dragon.

Creative mode – Game mode where players can create and build their own world using raw materials. Players have unlimited resources.

Survival mode – Game mode where players fight hostile mobs such as Creeper. Players have limited health and resources.

Creeper – Some weird green dude who is a bit of a killing machine. He sneaks up on the player and explodes in a stealth attack.

Bedrock – A rock that cannot be broken unless in creative mode.

I couldn't believe that I understood every word that Alfie said! I felt pretty chuffed with myself. I can't actually play the game, mind you – Arthur made me try once after he designed a "new world". He wanted to see if I could defeat the bad guy. No less than three minutes after I started, the tablet was slowly and firmly withdrawn from my hands.

"Er, maybe I should just do that for you. It seems like you don't really understand basic and simple movements – like walking," Arthur said with absolute disdain.

The cheek of him! To be fair, I was utterly shit and I have no idea how people can walk using thumbs and fingers on a bloody screen. I need a joystick – but then I have no desire to get any good at *Minecraft*. I'm just happy I understand the lingo so I can comprehend what my boys are saying, and more importantly, I can communicate with them in their own language. I'm serious. Just using the *Minecraft* terminology causes my boys to listen and respond so much better than regular old English. I'll give you an example. "Right, guys, it's bedtime. We're in survival mode and the Ender Dragon is going to come looking for all the little boys in their beds if they are not asleep by eight o'clock!" Anytime I engage with my children using *Minecraft* lingo, I know they will listen, and I know they will smile. More often than not, they also do as they're told. It's a language well worth knowing if your kids are into this game.

But what other languages do we speak? We know way more than you'd think. For instance, you may have particular words that are of significance to a certain group, or a certain physical action that holds meaning only to those who are in on the joke. Language isn't just about the words spoken, but about how and why the words are connected, and the meaning they hold for us.

When navigating the early days of sobriety, the way we speak and the language we use is crucial. Getting sober really is like learning an entirely new lingo. Before I tried to quit drinking alcohol, I did not speak sobriety. I didn't know any of the language. I'd heard it was beautiful, but at that time, the thought of giving up drinking was too ridiculous a suggestion to entertain. I didn't care how wonderful the language was if I had to leave my best friend Pinot behind. I didn't want to know.

The first sober lingo I ever heard of was "quit lit". My first step towards learning the language of sobriety was to pick up a book about getting sober. I bought two. *Alcohol Lied to Me* by Craig Beck and *The Unexpected Joy of Being Sober* by Catherine Gray. I can't remember which one I read first, I just recall being utterly astounded at how much I didn't know and understand about alcohol. I highly recommend both of these books. Reading them was like lifting the proverbial veil – I would never look at alcohol the same way again. I quickly developed a new addiction – to "quit lit". I studied books, articles, blogs, medical journals and listened to podcasts and YouTube videos on addiction. I wanted to know everything. Knowledge truly is power – especially when it comes to any kind of addiction.

I often get emails from clients who are super hard on themselves. They can be a couple of months into sobriety and kicking themselves because they're still craving alcohol or seeing value in it. I tell everyone the same thing: "You're learning an entirely new language; it's not easy and it takes time." If you were to learn Mandarin, how long would it take for you to become fluent? A long time! Mandarin is, apparently, the hardest language in the world to learn, and yet it's also the second most spoken language globally. Over a billion people speak Mandarin, so, to a seventh of the world population, the language isn't difficult at all – yet to those starting to learn, it's seriously bloody difficult. It's a choice to learn and speak a new language continuously, until it eventually becomes part of your subconscious – that is, you speak fluently without even thinking about it – and then it becomes easy.

Do not expect to crack sobriety overnight. Be kind to yourself. It's okay to get cravings. It's normal to feel like you're missing out. That you've given something up. The first year involves a lot of "firsts". First Christmas, first holiday, first birthday and so on. And even then there will be challenges that you won't face for many months or even years – like coping with the death of someone close to you while sober.

It's okay to have a mental wobble and temporarily forget your sober language. A thought cannot make you drink. And having the thought does not mean you've failed. It's just par for the course. An inevitable stumble while learning any new language.

So, how do you learn to speak sobriety fluently? Same as you'd learn how to speak any other language. Read, learn and practise. If you put the time and effort into learning, just as you would if you wanted to speak Mandarin, you will eventually become fluent. It really is that simple. And I now know that sobriety truly is the most beautiful language there is.

Discovering Alcohol

Before alcohol even touched my lips for the first time, I was desperate to try it. I was an addict waiting to happen and an alcohol advertiser's perfect potential customer. I bought into alcohol long before I even knew how it felt or what it would do to me. Why? Because I was an impressionable and insecure teenage girl who quite simply wanted to rebel. I saw drinking before the legal age as the equivalent of giving my mum the middle finger.

I had a tempestuous relationship with my mum. We began to argue when I reached my teenage years, because I wanted to get out, see my friends, and generally become more independent. This was particularly difficult when my mum's favourite word was "no", and her qualification for why she said no was "because I said so". This response would fill me with nothing short of rage – the equivalent of pouring petrol on fire.

If I asked to stay out until ten in the evening (because that was the curfew for all of my friends), my mum would insist that I be home by nine. I don't believe her rationale had anything to do with wanting to keep me safe. I think she said no because she desperately wanted to try to show me that she was in control. In doing so, it only caused me to push back even harder.

In 1996, I was 14 years old and I had a small role in my school play. I have no memory of what the actual production was, just that I was playing a witch and I got to sing, which I absolutely loved. Singing was something that made me feel electric and alive. I was terrified of being on stage in front of people, but I had (and still have) an absolute addiction to the feeling of nervous excitement, that cocktail of chemical waves which ripple through your body.

My mum always described me as "fearless". I wasn't. I was a scared little lamb, but willing to try anything potentially frightening. It didn't come from a place of feeling brave. I now realize that my teenage ability to do something scary or even terrifying ironically came from a place of deep-rooted insecurity. I wanted to appear unafraid. That's what I wanted other people to see. I wanted people to call me fearless. I thought maybe if they did, it would eventually become true. I lived for the approval of others. I felt that my mum didn't like me and I constantly rebelled against her because, at least then, I got her attention. I just wanted to be loved. I went about getting it in the worst possible way.

The lead in the play was a 17-year-old girl in the sixth form. I was incredibly jealous that she had the best role and got to sing most of the songs, but she was lovely, and after the last performance, she invited the whole cast to her eighteenth birthday party. I was so excited to go. It was my first proper party, and it was 70s themed. I dressed up in a psychedelic top, hot pants and brown suede knee-high platform boots I'd borrowed from a neighbour. I battled with anorexia for most of high school, and I was crushingly insecure about my body, but my lack of confidence was heavily outweighed by the desire to look attractive for any boys at the party. I was especially excited because I knew I would be able to drink.

The party was held in a club hall that had been hired out for the evening and had a makeshift bar stocked with bottles of booze, such as Hooch, which were brightly coloured and had pictures on the side. These drinks were undoubtedly designed and marketed to get teenagers hooked. I opted for the lemon-flavoured Hooch and can still remember the taste, but more importantly, I vividly remember the feeling.

After a few sips of Hooch, I knew what I had been missing out on. This was the cure to everything that was wrong with me. I felt like someone had covered me in a soothing balm. All of my insecurities melted away, and I felt like the version of myself that I so desperately wanted to be: the fearless one. I didn't worry about how I looked anymore or what people thought of me. It was like slipping into a new skin that felt so much more comfortable than my own. Alcohol was definitely the answer.

After just one drink, I was already pretty tipsy. Firstly, because I was new to drinking, and secondly, because I was tiny. I didn't eat most of the time because I wanted to be smaller, but I never found a size that was "small enough" to make me happy. After just one drink, I started to lose my footing. The platform boots were high and difficult to walk in sober, and tipsy, I had no chance. I must have resembled Bambi trying to take his first steps. Still, I loved the woozy feeling, and I had no desire to slow down or stop drinking, so I had another.

I got drunk very quickly. After two drinks, I remember very little. I know there was dancing and someone drove me home, but that's about it. I woke up the next day feeling fine with no hangover, but very anxious. I had no idea what I had said or done the night before and, since I didn't have a mobile phone back then, I had to wait to find out. Luckily, I didn't have to wait too long as I saw my friends later that day. They told me that I had made a total fool of myself and that I had even licked a boy's face while dancing at some point. I was mortified.

On the following Monday, I went to school and clearly remember taking my reading glasses with me, even though I didn't need them. My vision was almost perfect, and I had only faked an eye test to get a pair of glasses because I thought they would look cool. I could barely see through the lenses, so I never used them. However, on that particular Monday, I wore them to school, hoping to appear smarter, and be seen as the studious geek that I normally was, rather than the drunken idiot I had become at the party.

Some of the other kids gave me grief by delightfully rehashing stories about me stumbling into walls and throwing myself at boys. This was my first taste of alcohol-related shame. I felt terrible. I wore my glasses, hoping they would have the same effect on me as they did on Superman – I'd become Clark Kent, totally unrecognizable by a simple disguise. Needless to say, I was unsuccessful. However, there were also great comments from some of the popular (troubled) kids who congratulated me on getting hammered and being a party girl who was fun.

You would think that my early experience with the indignity caused by drinking would have put me off, but obviously, it didn't. I wanted to be fearless again. I didn't feel anxious while I was drinking. My brain was constantly overwhelmed with thoughts of worthlessness, inadequacy and unattractiveness, and I craved the other version of me – the one who didn't give a shit. The one who felt attractive. I liked her. She was fearless, she was fun, and other people thought so too! Maybe I could even become more popular. All I needed to do was to pick up another drink. So, I did. And my drinking career began. Just like that.

Alcohol Causes Fun and Excitement, Right?

> "It's all fun and games until someone loses
> an eye, then it's just fun you can't see."

James Hetfield

One incredibly hot summer morning, I lay down on the bathroom floor to put my face on the cold tiles. I remember sweating profusely and feeling that awful sensation of saliva filling my mouth, a sure sign that I was about to vomit. I had been out with friends the night before and had consumed at least a couple of bottles of wine, probably more. My head throbbed with soul-crushing intensity, and the heat made it so much worse. I felt my stomach lurch, and I began to vomit violently, over and over, until all I was bringing up was green-coloured bile. I didn't just feel hungover; I felt like I was dying. The heat, extreme dehydration, stomach pains and pounding headache were a viscous cocktail of symptoms, and, like so many hungover days before, I wasn't entirely sure it was survivable.

I pulled myself up to my feet and washed my face with cold water, which provided a few seconds of relief. I looked in the mirror and was appalled at the haggard mess staring back at me. All I wanted to do was crawl back into bed. Only this was not my house; it belonged to a client – and I was at work.

After my eldest son was born, I decided that I needed a project, so I set up a small cleaning business alongside working full-time. Even before I became a mum, I always made sure I was busy. I love having a project on the go, and, if I'm not spinning multiple plates, I have a tendency to become bored. In my drinking days, boredom often led to self-destructive behaviour, so staying busy was preferable.

On this particular day, I was training a new cleaner and doing a deep clean of a five-bedroom house, which meant eight solid hours of work – bloody hard work. Even on a hangover-free day, a day-long deep clean would leave me exhausted and feeling like I'd just run a marathon. With a hangover, it was like crawling up Mount Everest on my hands and knees. Why did I do this to myself? I knew that I needed to be up early, and I knew that I needed to have loads of energy. I willingly threw back glass after glass of Pinot the night before, wildly and loudly declaring "FUCK IT!" when my friends mentioned that I should maybe slow down because they knew I needed to be up in the morning. The problem was, after even one drink, I didn't give a shit.

The prefrontal cortex of your brain, which is responsible for rational thinking and decision-making, becomes flawed when it has been lubricated by alcohol. When alcohol enters your bloodstream, it interrupts the normal functioning of your prefrontal cortex and you make decisions without considering the consequences. This is why, when you pick up your phone the morning after a session the night before, you can't believe the messages that you sent or how that person seems so far removed from who you actually are. It's not you. It's like you're in your body, but someone else is driving your brain – usually a total wanker.

That day of cleaning was purgatory. The girl I was training was only 20 years old, sprightly, full of energy, and didn't drink, because she was a semi-professional gymnast. I can remember thinking at the time that I wished I had spent my teenage years doing something that amazing – a hobby that didn't involve alcohol. I was in my mid-thirties and felt like a total hot mess, and here was this young girl who clearly had her shit together way more than I did. I felt sad, depressed and foolish. I went home exhausted and opened another bottle of wine. Hair of the dog was the only solution when I felt that bad.

I would like to say that I learned my lesson and never cleaned another house in such a shit state, but of course, I did – many times over. I made my life so fucking hard. To this day, I have no idea how I managed my crazy schedule while I was perpetually hungover. Each and every day was painful. Something to drag myself through. I lived for the evenings when I could melt the day away with a bottle of wine. I told myself that I could handle the daily slog because I always got my reward at the end of it. However long, tiring or exhausting my day was, I could always rely on wine to take the pain away. I always felt enlivened at the point of opening a bottle. My day rapidly improved and I became instantaneously spritely. And isn't that one of the reasons why we drink? It makes life that bit more exciting. Doesn't it?

I spent a huge amount of my time hungover and feeling fucking terrible. What is so good about alcohol that I felt bored to tears without it, and why did I look back with such fondness that I often struggled to remember why I quit in the first place? I wasted a lot of headspace ruminating on whether or not I had a problem with alcohol. Was my issue with wine really that bad? Most of my friends drank the same amount as I did. It wasn't as if I was physically dependent. I could have a day off! Maybe I was too hasty in saying I was going to quit forever. Perhaps I just needed a break from alcohol to feel healthier and reset.

The thing is, I spent many years "taking breaks". But I always went back – because I was addicted to it and needed wine to numb the intense anxiety that comes from, you know, the wine. So whenever my evil twin (the voice of the addict in my head) started to whisper to me about the prospect of an amazing life, drinking wine in moderation, I made a conscious decision to think about Dry January. If alcohol is so good, why do people all over the world give it up for January? Why do so many of us talk about needing to "cut down"? If wine is the wonderful, rose-tinted, fantastic and life-enhancing elixir, why do so many people want time off it?

I have never seen a blog or social media post where someone broke their sober streak and congratulated themselves for being back at day zero. Without exception, everyone who ends up back there feels self-loathing and disappointment. Upset that their hard work in building up precious days, months and even years of sobriety was wiped out so easily with one drink – and just like that – back to day zero. I have never heard someone who got back on to alcohol saying, "I had a year of sobriety, but now I'm so happy I'm drinking again every day! You should all give up quitting now! I don't know why I ever thought to give it up! Life as an addict is so much fun!"

I've come to notice that, more often than not, addicts are highly intelligent, incredibly successful people and consequently in need of huge amounts of mental stimulation. Overthinking and self-criticizing are common, and operating at an optimum level under pressure is both mentally and physically exhausting. If you've got more going on in your brain, you've basically got more shit you want to shut out. Alcohol can quickly induce calm and relaxation and give us the rush – the "high" – a lovely big shot of happy hormones.

When we have our first drink, the brain releases dopamine. This is one of the "feel-good" hormones. We feel instantly relieved of negative emotions. It only takes ten minutes for alcohol to kick in. It's rapid. That's one of the main reasons I drank – instant relief. The body reacts to the presence of alcohol and needs to achieve homeostasis – balance. The brain recognizes that it has unusually high levels of dopamine, so it seeks to bring those back into balance by releasing cortisol – the stress hormone. When you stop drinking, the dopamine begins to wear off and the cortisol remains. This is why we wake up feeling anxious in the night.

The brain becomes accustomed to alcohol consumption. It knows that it will get its dopamine release from booze – so it stops producing dopamine naturally. Your mind learns to wait for the alcohol, and when it doesn't get it, you get a craving, because it is hard-wired to seek out dopamine. This is why cravings feel like such an intense compulsion. It's instinctive. No different than a predator hunting for prey. When we quit drinking, it takes up to 90 days of sobriety for the brain to start firing up and producing dopamine on its own again. This is why early sobriety feels boring and unexciting – it's very hard to feel pleasure or joy in the first few weeks of being alcohol-free, simply because you're lacking in happy hormones.

For each glass of alcohol consumed, there is an increase in both dopamine and cortisol levels. Consequently, after consuming alcohol, one typically feels worse than before drinking. This is why drinking in moderation is as futile as drinking larger amounts of booze – even if you stop at one or two, you will end up feeling worse than you did before you started. If you're drinking to relax, you will only feel better for the first 20 to 40 minutes, and the trade-off is that once you finish, you wind up in a worse emotional state than when you started. It's pointless.

It's easy to conclude that sobriety is boring due to the lack of happy hormones in the early stages of quitting booze. Similarly, it's easy to assume that drinking alcohol must be the cause of excitement and fun because, without it, life feels tedious and monotonous. The reality is that enjoyment comes from being with people you love and doing fun things. Alcohol is, in fact, a depressant and there is nothing in a bottle that can cause actual happiness. It's an illusion. When we drink, we get a temporary dopamine spike, numb ourselves to our problems and care less about the issues we're facing. Why? Because booze simultaneously slows down the central nervous system and brain function, creating an analgesic effect. The temporary absence of negative feelings may be equated with happiness, but the problems remain when we wake up the next day, and we often feel worse. If alcohol causes so much fun and happiness, shouldn't it follow that more alcohol equals more happiness?

Alcohol is a numbing agent that deadens not only the bad emotions but also the good ones, including true experiences of joy and happiness. When you are sober, you can address your problems and actually feel the good emotions, allowing you to enjoy them fully. Alcohol makes all problems feel so much worse, so by not drinking in the first place, your issues will never seem as significant. Quitting alcohol is a really great way to gain a much better, positive perspective on all the problems you currently face. Sober, it's also far easier to find the solutions.

Seeking Approval

"If you live for people's acceptance, you will die from their rejection."

Lecrae

Although I may have been a rebel at home, I was always well behaved and studious at school, finding the work relatively easy and enjoyable. I was a straight-A student. After I discovered alcohol, it was as if my personality split in two. During the week, I would work hard, but on weekends, I would go wild. I began going to nightclubs at the age of 15 and my mum lost all control over me. She reluctantly allowed me to go out as long as she could pick me up at the end of the night, no matter how late. Looking back, I think she must have been terrified. I would dress in the skimpiest outfit I could find, get completely blasted, and she would drive into Chester town centre to peel me off the pavement and get me home safely.

Most nights, I would walk into a club and order eight shots of tequila during happy hour, with the mission of getting as drunk as possible, as quickly as possible. I would slam the shots one after the other and then spend about 30 minutes in agony in the bathroom, as my stomach throbbed and pulsed in pain. It was an awful half-hour, but it would end with instant drunkenness and the wrenching in my belly would slide away. I would then spend the rest of the night with my friends – throwing myself around the dance floor and trying to hook up with boys. I would inevitably end up kissing some random boy (or man) and get his home telephone number on a bar napkin (yeah – I'm that old!). I would then wait for my mum to pick me up. Nine times out of ten, I would spend the night throwing up, and the next day hanging out of my arse.

I started working as a paper delivery girl when I was 12, and I've never been out of work since – a work ethic instilled in me by my dad. I started working at weekends when I was just 13 years old, as a waitress, chambermaid, salesgirl, and held many other jobs over the years – 24 to be exact! I wanted my own money desperately because it gave me freedom. I needed money so I could go out and drink, spending every penny I earned on slutty outfits and alcohol.

Every Saturday and Sunday, I would get up for work and slog through my day, totally hungover. I have no idea how I actually managed to do this. There were many days when I would find myself in the work toilets, bringing up green bile because I'd been sick so much that that was all that was left. I tolerated the hangover because the alternative wasn't an option: staying sober on a Friday and Saturday night. Er, I don't fucking think so.

I didn't see that I was doing anything wrong or dangerous. All of my friends did the same. We worshipped the Spice Girls, and we grew up during a significant period of worldwide female rebellion. My late teens and the whole of my twenties were spent getting hammered and sleeping around. I have never had a one-night stand sober – but I've had a frightening number of one-night stands. I thankfully lost count many years ago, as I'm sure I'd be pretty horrified if I knew the actual figure.

Alcohol and sleeping around went hand in hand for me. I drank to escape my crushing insecurities and become another version of myself, a version I believed was better. Male attention made me feel wanted, even if it was just for the night. Secondary to alcohol, sleeping around was a futile attempt to make me feel good about myself. Funnily enough, I only ever felt worse. I never spent a period of time on my own; I was either sleeping around or hopping from relationship to relationship. Ever since I was 15 years old, I've felt I needed the validation of a man. It's heart-breaking to write this. I feel terrible for my younger self. Since I became sober, I don't look back and see that girl as me. It's like looking through a lens at someone else. I feel sorry for her and wish I could go back in time and give her a massive hug and some sound advice.

I got married when I was 29 years old, to a friend who became my partner. To me, he seemed safe and secure. All of my relationships before my husband were tempestuous and volatile, but also passionate. I convinced myself that in order to get the life I wanted (the Disney version), I needed to be with someone who didn't start off as a one-night stand. I couldn't be with someone who I was infatuated with from the off, as those relationships were impossible for me to sustain. I was married for almost a decade before it became glaringly apparent that the lack of spark between us was palpable and impossible to ignore. I'm not going to talk about the issues in my marriage, or the many reasons for its ultimate demise, largely because my boys may one day read this book – but when I eventually left, I was relieved and devastated in equal measure. I had to destroy my family unit in order to find happiness. I wanted my boys to have a life where their parents stayed together, like I had, but I was deeply unhappy, and the only thing worse than leaving was staying.

When I left my husband, I was still drinking. The divorce quickly became acrimonious, as they generally do. My lawyer said to me early on in the process, "There is no such thing as a civil divorce." Yeah – go figure. Thankfully, my ex-husband and I now get along and co-parent well. We're on the same page with raising our boys and our relationship is courteous. I'm very grateful for this. During the divorce, however, I was the most stressed out that I've ever been. I was plagued with financial worries and feared that I would lose my home and not be able to support my children. All I could do to stamp out those thoughts was to drink heavily. I drank almost every night, desperate to feel nothing, even if it was just for a few hours a day. It was during my year-long divorce that I decided to quit drinking. I knew that I couldn't make good decisions for my own or my children's future while I was so desperately unhealthy and living in abject chaos.

I jumped straight out of a ten-year marriage and into a long-term relationship – while I was separated, drinking heavily and at my absolute worst. "Out of the frying pan and into the fire" just about sums it up. I met a man online and dived head first into being fully committed. The first online date I ever went on resulted in a relationship that lasted over a year and a half. Despite the initial attraction, he was fundamentally wrong for me. We didn't want the same things and I didn't get anything I needed from him emotionally. To me it seemed that he was very selfish and his own needs didn't just come first, they were the only needs that were ever considered. I felt he was unavailable in every sense and, despite being in a relationship, I was perpetually lonely. I stayed because, once again, I found myself scared of being by myself – of feeling unloved and unwanted, which was ironic because I felt unloved and unwanted, even when I was with him.

I got sober about four months into dating him, and I started to question what the hell I was doing. I knew I would eventually leave and I journalled about it all the time. I even left a few times, but I kept going back – knowing that I would be miserable either way, so I felt like it was better to be miserable and at least feel like I was desired. The lesser of two evils – because I couldn't handle being alone. But my internal voice would not shut up! She told me over and over that I was not happy and not where I wanted to be. It was like being constantly nagged from the inside out. Sober, I couldn't shut that voice off. It got louder and louder until it was eventually screaming at me. I had to listen. Without alcohol, it was impossible to ignore forever. It took a great deal of soul-searching before I finally realized that I needed to honour my internal voice and that being alone was actually the final piece of my sobriety puzzle. Being able to be entirely independent, both literally and emotionally, was the one thing I was missing.

Sobriety has allowed me to focus on what I want and need from my life. I now describe myself as "single and unavailable". I don't require validation from a man to be happy and I'm choosing to stay single for now, because I'm still working on finding out who I am and what I really want from my life. I'm simply not interested in dating. I certainly won't be going online, and if I do eventually meet someone, it will be organically. If I don't, I'm fine with that too. What will be will be.

Alcohol dependency is rarely the only problem. When you're reliant on a substance to change the way you feel, you're also likely to be looking for outside validation or using other crutches. One of the greatest benefits of sobriety is that your internal voice becomes LOUD. She is the voice that represents your deepest wants and desires. She is a powerhouse of a woman, desperate to be heard. When I drank, I spent a lifetime trying to get her to shut the fuck up. Now that I'm sober, I've realized that the only true route to happiness is to listen to her. She knows what I want, what I need, and because I am sober, she helps me make good choices.

My relationship with men has historically been exactly the same as the relationship I had with alcohol: dependent. Now that I'm free from alcohol dependency, I want to be fully independent in all other areas of my life too. Finding out what I love, what makes me joyful, and spending time with my friends and family is crucial for my mental health and happiness. I've realized that while it can feel great to have a partner, I feel love from so many other sources, including myself. I have the most incredible support system, and I couldn't wish for better friends and family. My boys are an endless source of joy, and our love is completely unconditional – both ways. I have three men in my life – my dad and my two boys – and they're the only ones I need.

Thanks to sobriety, I'm alone for the first time since I was 15 years old – and I've never felt more complete.

The Four Stages of Alcoholism

> "If you see you're going to win, you're going to celebrate."

Usain Bolt

I don't believe scaremongering gets anyone to quit alcohol. The worst-case scenario is death. We all know this. You can't get much scarier than that. So why is it that the dangers of drinking aren't enough to stop most people from picking up a glass?

Way before I ever picked up my first "quit lit" book, I knew that alcohol was slowly killing me. I had deep-rooted anxiety about the functionality of my liver. I can remember reading something in the news many years ago that said if you have 25 per cent liver function remaining, after two months off alcohol, your liver can completely regenerate. But if over 75 per cent of the liver is damaged, there is no coming back from that. Liver cirrhosis territory. I often wondered about what percentage I was at. I was genuinely worried that my liver was basically just a ticking time bomb and I was actually fairly surprised that it hadn't already spontaneously combusted. The liver has no nerve endings, so it can't tell you when it's fucked. By the time you get symptoms of cirrhosis, it's often too late. What if I was past the point of no return? I was terrified of the possibility, but the fear of this did not stop me drinking. Knowledge of the dangers did not make me put down the glass. I felt the fear and did it anyway – and not in a good way.

Understanding what alcohol is, what it does and the damage it causes is essential to unravelling the widely held false beliefs that exist and are endorsed by society. But the issue with focusing on this and this alone is that you stay fixated on fear. Fear-induced sobriety is rarely successful. Fear didn't stop me drinking. It was something much more powerful that made me successful: hope.

I spent a lifetime trying desperately to moderate because I was scared of the consequences of not doing so. But what I missed completely was what I could gain by getting sober – the benefits. The hope of an incredible, beautiful, healthy future. Fear was the driver to quit, but it was the promise of a much better future that allowed me to maintain it. When we're goal-focused and work towards what we want, rather than what we don't want, we can take inspired action to get there, one baby step at a time.

Think about this: when an athlete is training for a sports event, they don't focus on the times they failed or the pain of losing. They focus, imagine and visualize winning. When Usain Bolt is on the starting blocks before a race, do you think he is thinking about how dreadful it felt every time he lost before? He isn't thinking about where he doesn't want to be. One hundred per cent of his focus is on where he wants to end up – crossing the finish line and winning. The same goes for getting sober.

That said, it is helpful to know where you are on the timeline to physical dependence so you have a clear indication of where your starting block begins. Sticking your head in the sand is dangerous. We need to be educated about what happens on the descent into alcoholism so we can be honest with ourselves about how bad our problem is. It can form a very important part of the decision to quit, how we quit and serve as a catalyst for taking the necessary steps to get where we want and need to be.

There isn't a definitive point, day or moment where someone hits the point of no return. When I say "the point of no return", I'm referring to irreparable liver cirrhosis and other incurable health conditions. There isn't a doctor in the land who can tell you at which exact moment you will hit physical dependence, over and above problem drinking. But there are solid indicators and evidence-based stages. By knowing what stage you are at, you can understand the severity of your own situation. Hopefully, in facing this, you can see the monumental value of changing and quitting for good.

I'm not explaining the stages of alcoholism to scare anyone. I believe it's vital to understand the facts in order to understand the gravity of the problem you're facing. Sometimes just lifting the veil and providing clarity can give us "that" moment – the moment every sober person on the planet once had, the moment they chose to stop for good and went on to succeed.

The four stages of alcoholism

Elvin Morton Jellinek was a scientist who specialized in alcohol addiction research in the 1960s. He published several papers on the progressive nature of alcoholism, theorizing that problem drinking follows four stages of decline and categorizing each one by the behaviours exhibited by drinkers in each phase. Jellinek does subscribe to the "disease model of addiction" theory, which I do not at all, but the stages of alcoholism make sense to me irrespective of this. (I will cover the disease model of addiction theory in the chapter Why Is it so Hard to Find Out How to Quit?, but in a nutshell, it suggests that alcohol is not the problem – you are. You have a disease that stops you from being able to moderate like *normal* people.) Jellinek's studies and publications eventually led to the formation of the Jellinek Curve, which illustrates the symptoms seen during a person's progression through the stages of alcoholism:

- *Pre-alcoholic stage*
- *Early-stage alcoholism*
- *Middle alcoholic phase*
- *End-stage alcoholism*

I have used Jellinek's model as the basis for my layman's explanation of each of the four stages. There are no time limits, and the stages can occur slowly over many years or rapidly over just a few weeks.

Pre-alcoholic (stage one)

At this stage, drinking isn't causing problems, and it isn't compulsive. This category includes ANYONE who drinks any amount of alcohol, however small. Why is a person who consumes even a small amount of alcohol considered a pre-alcoholic? Because anyone at this stage is using alcohol to change how they feel. The more a person drinks, the more dependent they become on ethanol. It's that simple. If you use alcohol to change how you feel for the small stressors in life, your brain begins to rewire to see alcohol as the solution for all stressful situations. Drinking at this stage is generally social, and it's not regular. Pre-alcoholics just use a little alcohol for perceived relaxation, to unwind, deal with difficult emotions or de-stress at the end of a day. Seeking treatment during this stage is highly unlikely.

Early-stage alcoholism (stage two)

Early-stage alcoholism is characterized by regular binge drinking, which can result in occasional blackouts. Binge drinking is defined differently across the globe. Put simply, it's having a lot of alcohol in a short space of time. In the UK, it's defined as consuming six units or more in a single session for women, and eight units or more within a single session for men. (A unit is defined as containing ten millilitres or eight grams of pure alcohol – so evidently the type of drink will change this figure significantly.) As a rough guide, that's the equivalent of about four pints of average strength beer for a man, or three pints for a woman. Enjoying rapid onset drunkenness, that is drinking with the intention of getting drunk, may be indicative of a deeper problem.

In early-stage alcoholism, the frequency of drinking is high, but not daily. Individuals in this stage simply cannot imagine having a good social night out without alcohol. The following mantras are often used to justify heavy drinking sessions: "I just want to socialize and have a good time", "I just want to relax", "I can have days off easily" and "I can take it or leave it".

Individuals in stage two are already preparing for a serious problem with alcohol. They may joke about drinking to excess or behaving out of character when drinking. This cycle often involves drinking heavily, passing out, swearing to cut back, abstaining for a while, and then repeating the cycle.

Middle alcoholic phase (stage three)

This was the stage I was at when I decided to quit drinking for good. Friends and family of stage three drinkers may begin to notice changes in their behaviour and start commenting on their drinking. Drinkers at this stage may lie about how much they drink and become highly skilled at hiding it, even from themselves.

The consequences of drinking become more apparent, with regular hangovers, anxiety, waking up in the middle of the night and cravings for alcohol. Middle alcoholics become irritable and find themselves drinking more to achieve the same effect.

They experience frequent blackouts or memory lapses, sallow skin, blemishes, stomach problems and other ailments. They may choose to drink over engaging in other activities, and their relationships may suffer due to changes in behaviour when drunk, such as becoming insulting towards loved ones, causing arguments or frequently showing up for work hungover. There is often a lot of self-hatred, desperation to change, and repeated attempts to cut down or quit. Some people may even announce they have a problem.

Stage three drinkers who try to quit regularly find themselves back at "day one". While they can sometimes abstain for sustained periods of time, usually between two days and two months, they generally return to drinking, often consuming more than before. This stage is when most people realize they need treatment and begin to seek it. A stage three drinker's health is not beyond repair, and with guidance and help, they are capable of making significant changes, becoming healthy and achieving lifelong sobriety.

End-stage alcoholism (stage four)

Before I picked up a "quit lit" book, I stereotypically viewed an alcoholic as someone in the end-stage of alcoholism. In this final stage, the effects of alcohol consumption become glaringly obvious and take priority over everything else. Those in stage four may have attempted to cut down or quit many times before, spanning weeks or even years. All-day drinking is common at this stage, and some (but not all) may take their first "morning drink". Physical dependence becomes severe, and attempting to stop abruptly could result in seizures or even death. Therefore, supervised detox is essential for safety, and quitting alone is extremely difficult. Life is hugely impacted, and relationships, work and finances can suffer significantly. While some people may continue to function highly, they often experience excruciating anxiety when not drinking, and their health may be at significant risk, including liver failure and cancer.

The aim of presenting this timeline is to emphasize that individuals in stage two or three of alcoholism are only ever potentially a few weeks away from stage four – especially if triggered by a single significant life event or trauma. This is why even minimal alcohol consumption can be risky. My dad is a perfect example; he went from a stage two drinker to a stage four drinker within three weeks when my mum suddenly died. I quit at stage three, never believing I would get to stage four – until I lost my mum and got divorced in the same year. Those two events caused my drinking to increase rapidly and my tolerance for alcohol to skyrocket. Fortunately, with therapy, I managed to pull myself out before hitting end-stage alcoholism, but it was looming like a black cloud. No drinker is exempt from the risks of consuming alcohol.

Life's challenges are inevitable, and we never know when they might strike. If you're fortunate enough to be in the early stages of alcoholism, it's the perfect opportunity to break free from the grip of addiction. Otherwise, there's a risk of a slow and organic descent into alcoholism, or a significant life event causing your drinking to escalate rapidly. The human body is an incredible machine and can recover swiftly from alcoholism. In just a few weeks after quitting, the body can reverse a remarkable amount of damage. So having reviewed the stages of alcoholism, let's now explore a beautiful timeline: what happens when you stop drinking.

What Happens When You Stop Drinking – the Timeline

> "The journey of a thousand miles begins with a single step."

Lao Tzu

When we drink, we are all too familiar with the predictable timeline. Some days we stop before the chaos, sickness and blackouts occur, but we know that continuing to drink will only lead to a bad ending. We know that each stage is predictable and the timeline of events usually plays out like so.

1. *As soon as we take the first sip, we feel an instant sense of relaxation, and our troubles seem less important. Even if we plan to have only one drink, the prefrontal cortex (the decision-making part of our brain) starts to change. With just one drink, our rational thinking begins to fade, and the "fuck-it button" takes over, urging us to have another.*

2. *After two drinks, we become louder, more "confident", and convinced that we are funnier, more charming and sexier. However, our perception of ourselves and how others perceive us can be vastly different.*

3. *We keep drinking until we begin to slur our words.*

4. *Our coordination starts to decline, starting with our speech and then our body. We become clumsy and lose fine motor control.*

5. *Our behaviour becomes incongruous with our values. Sometimes we end up offending people.*

6. *We vomit.*

7. *We either black out or lose consciousness.*

8. *We wake up in the middle of the night with heart palpitations, anxiety, self-loathing and a throbbing headache.*

9. *We feel hungover.*

10. *We struggle through the day, feeling terrible, until our brain craves dopamine again, and the cycle repeats.*

We can all relate to the alcohol timeline. It happens every time we drink, and the only real variable is how far we progress along that timeline. The great news is that the journey to sobriety follows the same predictable pattern!

There is a clear timeline for giving up alcohol, but if you've never read any "quit lit" books, you may not be aware of it. I certainly wasn't. I had no idea how long it would take for my body to heal from alcohol abuse or what the process would involve. I was completely oblivious to the physiological and mental impact of quitting drinking. I didn't know that it takes about three months to feel the full benefits of sobriety and return to a "normal" state. As they say, knowledge is power, and this couldn't be truer in relation to the journey to sobriety. If you know what to expect when you quit alcohol, if you understand what is happening to your body, and if you're aware that there is a process with a timeline, it's much easier to navigate.

For example, many people give up quitting between weeks four and eight because they conclude that sobriety is boring. If you're unaware of the facts around dopamine production, it's easy to deduce that alcohol causes happiness and sobriety is painfully dull. Armed with the facts, you can deal with each phase and appreciate them for what they are: transient.

Think of the journey to sobriety as a long, dark tunnel with a beginning, a middle and an end. Without knowledge of the quitting timeline, it's easy to crawl a few feet into a dark, dingy tunnel and conclude that it's awful and not worth it, so you'd rather go back and stay on the side you know and understand. But once you know what that tunnel looks like, what's inside there and how long it takes to reach the end, it's much easier to persevere. There is an end, and it's a glorious one.

The timeline for quitting is the same for everyone, although, much like drinking, some people will move faster along than others and may miss out on certain stages entirely. However, for those of you who may be physically dependent, it is important to seek advice from your doctor before you stop, as suddenly quitting can be dangerous and, in some cases, even fatal.

The good news is that the stages are predictable and fairly textbook. Once you become familiar with them, it's so much easier to quit because there is a reason for everything you will think and feel along your journey. There is safety in predictability. If you can see yourself at each stage and pinpoint yourself moving along the timeline, you can also see the most crucial element of this – it has an end. Put simply, you will not feel awful forever. Simple awareness of the timeline gives you control over it. How cool is that!

So, here's what to expect if you quit the wretched poison for good. Of course, each person will respond slightly differently. But what is certain is that for anyone and everyone who quits, everything will improve, and I mean everything – physically, mentally and socially. There isn't an area of your life that won't be affected for the better.

Days one to ten – withdrawal

At the time of quitting, I thought that having one day off each week was proof that I wasn't a real alcoholic. Of course, I was in denial – I just hadn't reached the physically dependent stage yet. I wasn't far off, though. About a month before I gave up, I was on holiday, so I had the perfect excuse to legitimately drink in the morning – a line I wouldn't ordinarily cross (aside from Christmas day, of course). By ten in the morning, I had a mimosa in hand, and I was acutely aware that I really wanted that morning drink. I felt extraordinarily anxious until I got alcohol into my system. I knew at that point that giving up would be a major challenge. Alcohol withdrawal usually lasts between three and seven days from the time of your last drink – but can be a little longer. What withdrawal looks like is entirely dependent on each individual person. For a great deal of people, alcohol withdrawal can be relatively mild, often presenting as irritability and a feeling like something is "missing". The withdrawal symptoms for me were unpleasant, but not horrendous by any stretch. Sweating, anxiety, being unable to sit still, unable to sleep and general restlessness were some of the symptoms I experienced. There was no physical pain; it was just uncomfortable. Rest assured, this stage only lasts a few short days, and then that first hurdle is overcome. From there on out, it's all down to what's going on in your head – and that is something that can be easily surmounted once you realize that you're not giving anything up at all. On the contrary, you're releasing yourself from a prison – a perpetual cycle of drinking, anxiety and self-hatred. Anyone can tolerate a few days of being uncomfortable in exchange for a life of abundant joy.

Of course, the early stages of withdrawal are not the same for everyone. Someone at stage four may well require detox within a facility or, at the very least, supported detox at home. If you're a daily dependent drinker, meaning you can't take a single day off alcohol without suffering withdrawal symptoms, it's really important not to quit alone and to be under the supervision of a medical professional.

If you can take days off alcohol, the withdrawal process really isn't that hard. I know this is a big statement, but think about what you actually feel on the days when you can't have a drink. When you focus on what happens in your mind and body, it's not physically painful when you don't drink; it's a mental itch.

Not drinking can make you feel unsettled, irritated, or downright angry, but it is entirely bearable, and it doesn't last long.

If you want to quit alcohol, the first three to five days are by far the hardest, but they're absolutely manageable. You just have to grind it out. Those first few days are in no way representative of what sobriety feels like in the long run. Withdrawal feels a lot like anxiety, and the symptoms are strikingly similar. For 25 years, I thought I was a very anxious person. Turns out, I'm not. I journalled throughout my quitting journey and rated both my anxiety and depression scores out of ten. Within a week of quitting drinking, my anxiety levels went from a whopping ten out of ten to three out of ten. I still have the odd day where something stressful happens and my scores increase a little, but that soul-crushing, want-to-rip-my-own-skin-off-to-get-out-of-my-body anxiety – it's gone. One week off alcohol, and I realized that my "anxiety" was actually just perpetual withdrawal.

Withdrawal symptoms end, just like that. Ten short days in, and your body is rid of the toxin. Physical cravings stop. Of course, the mental cravings may remain, but these are so much easier to manage. Once your brain stops seeking out dopamine, like a cat hunting a mouse, a craving is really no more than a mental desire that can easily be squashed with some simple coping mechanisms.

Ten days after quitting

Sleep improves drastically. Aah, shut-eye. No more alcohol-induced sleep coma. You are supposed to have between six and seven cycles of REM (rapid eye movement) sleep a night. Alcohol consumption reduces this to just one or two (I'll explain more on this later on pages 91–96). One week into sobriety, and you'll likely be sleeping like a baby. There is nothing quite like eight solid hours of blissful sleep with no interruptions. No need to get up to go to the bathroom. No waking up with anxiety and palpitations. No headache in the night. No need to glug a pint of water and pop paracetamol. Bliss!

There are so many benefits to getting better sleep. You will be more productive, and your problem-solving skills will improve. You'll be sharper and "on the ball". Your ability to control your emotions and behaviour will also improve. You'll also find it far easier to manage your food and drink intake. Good quality sleep helps to balance the hormones that make you feel hungry or full. After consuming alcohol, your ghrelin levels (the hormone that makes you feel hungry) increase, and leptin (the hormone that makes you feel full) decreases. Result!

Week two – hello, hydration! (and other lovely health benefits)

When you consume ethanol, you lose approximately four times as much liquid as you actually consumed – because it's a diuretic. This is why, once you start drinking and "break the seal", you need to pee so frequently, including during the night. Dehydration causes the dreaded hangover headache because your organs take water from the brain due to their own water loss. Additionally, salt and potassium levels decrease, which can impact nerve and muscle function, while also causing headaches, fatigue and nausea. Googling images of "the alcoholic brain" is super grim but absolutely fascinating. Have a look for yourself; it's an eye-opener to say the least – it looks a bit like a shrivelled sea creature. When I was drinking, I used to joke and say, "I can feel my brain shrinking" after a heavy night. Little did I know that it actually was. A few short days into quitting, you'll start repairing the damage, and your body can retain water again. The physical effects of this are amazing. Before you even reach two weeks sober, you can see a significant difference in your skin.

Hydration can also reduce eczema and dandruff. When I first quit drinking, after two weeks, my face looked positively glowing. Increased body water content meant my skin looked fresh and plump, had reduced redness, and my eyes became whiter and brighter. People will comment on the change in your appearance. It's positively palpable. It's basically like Botox, a skin peel and a mini-facelift – all for the price of… nothing! Just giving up a poisonous habit.

Alcohol is a pretty nasty irritant and damages the stomach lining. You will also see a rapid reduction in symptoms such as acid reflux, IBS and bloating. As I mentioned, I suffer from ulcerative colitis, and when I quit drinking, the improvement of my condition and associated symptoms was astounding. If you have any stomach issues or other ailments, sobriety will undoubtedly improve them.

Weeks one to four – sugar cravings

When I first quit, by day two, the sugar cravings came. I had believed up until this point that I didn't have a sweet tooth, but actually, I was just getting such huge quantities of sugar from alcohol (wine) that my body didn't crave it any more. I finally understand why wine drinkers opt for cheese and biscuits over pudding! They've already got their sugar hit! I craved sugar as I imagine a crack addict craves rocks – I was completely insatiable. In week two of my sober journey, I consumed 27 giant cookies in one sitting. I only stopped because I felt horribly sick!

Sugar is obviously not good for anyone's diet, but it's a damn sight better than drinking and a great form of harm reduction in those early days of sobriety, providing you don't have a health condition which limits your sugar intake and your doctor doesn't advise otherwise. (This is covered more in the chapter Harm Reduction – and the Dangers of Switching One Addiction for Another.) If you get a craving for alcohol, sugar can help to curb it. It sets off the dopamine receptors in the brain – not to the same degree as alcohol, but it does take the edge off. And anything that can do that in early sobriety is more than welcome in my book. However, this is a short-term fix. I advise all my clients that exercise and nutrition are both very important to achieving long-term sobriety and good health in general – not to mention that continued heavy intake of sugar can cause all manner of health conditions and diseases.

Weeks two to four – pink cloud

Around the end of week two, your body has rid itself of alcohol completely, you will have slept properly for the first time in years, and the irritability starts to ebb away to nothing. You will feel healthier, calmer and more peaceful than you can imagine. Two weeks into sobriety, a phenomenon called "pink cloud" happens as a result of these huge changes. I had not heard of pink cloud before I quit drinking. Someone mentioned it in a Facebook group, and I had to google it. Pink cloud describes the stage in early sobriety where recovering addicts develop feelings of euphoria and elation due to newfound excitement about the benefits of recovery, and their recently acquired elevated confidence in their ability to maintain abstinence. Put simply, you feel awesome – but unfortunately, it does not last forever.

Common feelings and experiences include:

- *Feelings of euphoria and extreme joy*
- *A hopeful outlook*
- *Positivity and optimism about recovery*
- *A calm or peaceful state of mind*
- *Confidence about your ability to maintain sobriety*
- *Preoccupation with the positive aspects of recovery*
- *Commitment to positive lifestyle changes*
- *Increased emotional awareness*

- *A tendency to overlook the hard work necessary to maintain sobriety*

So why does pink cloud happen? Some researchers believe it occurs because the body comes out of a state of withdrawal, and it's a symptom of relief now that the body is starting to heal. For me, hitting pink cloud was a delightful experience. I felt optimism and a drive for life that I had not felt in years. It was like I could suddenly see all the possibilities and potential for my life, an enthusiasm I only usually felt when aiming to get to the shop to buy wine before it closed. I felt fantastic. I couldn't believe that just removing alcohol from my life could feel that good!

The benefits of pink cloud are that you get a glimpse of what extended sobriety can feel like. You get a solid boost after the dreaded withdrawal period, and it can really spur you on to keep going. How do you know you're in pink cloud? For me, it was when I started to annoy my friends! When you feel that great, it's hard not to wax lyrical about it to anyone who will listen. I did not want to preach about sobriety or try to force other people to quit, but I felt so fantastic that I just wanted to share my new secret with anyone and everyone. I went overboard. I started to see some eye-rolling and realized it was probably time to shut my mouth.

The problem with pink cloud is that it's a transient state. It's wonderful, but it does not last long. For most people, it only lasts a few days to a few weeks. Some very lucky people hang out in this state for a few months apparently – but I have not met one of these elusive people before. What follows pink cloud is a crash, often with a nasty bump at the bottom. When you feel "high", much like being in the state of addiction, there is an inevitable low that follows. Sobriety requires internal work and self-discovery. This does not happen overnight. So, what follows pink cloud? Exhaustion.

Weeks one to six – the narcolepsy phase

If you've had a child, how tired did you feel in the first trimester of pregnancy? Just tired? Or soul-crushing exhaustion? This is what early sobriety feels like. When the body is using all its energy to grow a little human, your energy levels are massively depleted. When you're recovering from alcohol damage, the body is similarly using all its energy to heal. After sitting on top of the beautiful pink cloud, blissfully marvelling at the beauty of the world and all its possibilities, I crashed to the ground with an almighty thud. The only other time I can remember feeling this tired was when I first had my children and was breastfeeding. However, the difference with sobriety was I was actually sleeping. A lot. I went to bed early, got up late and napped in between. This was a cycle I remained in for about six weeks. It's a long time to feel like you're lacking in energy, and I certainly found myself getting increasingly despondent.

So why does the body become so exhausted in recovery? As already covered, when we drink, we miss out on the REM stage of sleep. When we're sober, we actually sleep properly – and this is the time when the body heals. It's no wonder that quitting alcohol is so exhausting really – the body has a huge amount of recuperation to do. I drank for a long time, so I viewed my six weeks of narcolepsy in early sobriety as catching up on 25 years of poor sleep!

The key to getting through this period of exhaustion is firstly understanding its place on the timeline, and knowing that it has an end – a "this too shall pass" kind of thing. Secondly, I highly recommend listening to your body and taking the rest when you need to. Fighting it is futile. You'll only wind up more exhausted. Believe me, I tried. You can do lots of things to look after yourself. Sleep, eat nutrition-rich food (in addition to the copious amounts of sugar!), get natural sunlight (even if it's just a very short daily walk), practise self-care and take vitamins. The basics. This is something I always come back to, time and time again. This doesn't just work for early sobriety but any time in life when you hit overwhelm. Go back to basics. Sleep, sunlight, good nutrition, exercise and social connection are the foundations for a happy and healthy existence. If you get this right, everything else will follow, and more importantly, everything else can wait.

Weeks two to four – the nightmare phase – literally

Research has shown, and you no doubt have personal experience of this, that drinking to excess causes you to fall asleep super-fast. I have certainly had many nights where I've crashed into bed and passed out just a few seconds after my head hit the pillow – hello, coma! Liver enzymes metabolize alcohol while we sleep, blood alcohol levels decrease, and sleep becomes incredibly disrupted. Sleep quality after consuming alcohol is basically just bloody awful – cue restlessness, intermittent waking, tossing and turning, and excessive sweating – to name just a few of the horrible symptoms.

To understand how alcohol impacts sleep, it is important to understand the various phases of the human sleep cycle. An alcohol-free sleep cycle has four different stages: three non-rapid eye movement (NREM) stages and one REM stage.

Stage 1 (NREM)

This is the period between wakefulness and sleep during which the body starts to rest. Heartbeat and breathing slow down as the muscles in the body relax.

Stage 2 (NREM)

Heartbeat and breathing rates continue to slow, and sleep begins to deepen. Body temperature decreases, and the eyes become still.

Stage 3 (NREM)

Heartbeat, breathing rates and brain activity all reach their lowest levels of the sleep cycle. Eye movements cease, and the muscles become totally relaxed.

Stage 4 (REM)

REM sleep begins about an hour and a half after sleep begins. This is the stage where dreaming takes place, and memories consolidate during REM sleep.

These four NREM and REM stages repeat in cycles throughout the night.

Alcohol is a sedative, making it easy to fall into a deep sleep quickly. However, as the night progresses, it creates an imbalance that leads to much less REM sleep and disrupts sleep cycles. Since REM sleep is when we get our best, dream-inducing sleep, we rarely experience heavy dreaming after drinking and never wake up feeling well rested. As alcohol wears off, the hormone dopamine also diminishes. During drinking, dopamine is counteracted by the release of cortisol – the stress hormone. Cortisol, combined with a lack of REM sleep, can result in waking up in the middle of the night feeling hyper-anxious. This is why, after a night of heavy drinking, you're almost guaranteed to wake up feeling like shit.

In early sobriety, I experienced the most incredible sleep for the first time in years, as my natural REM sleep cycle fired back up again. Having spent years with insomnia, disrupted sleep cycles and waking up with alcohol guilt, it was an absolute treat to be able to sleep solidly through the night again. Since week one of quitting booze, my sleep quality has improved 100 per cent. When I craved a glass of wine in early sobriety, I reminded myself that I would certainly wake up in the middle of the night with crippling anxiety, which was a really good incentive to stay off booze, because I now love getting some decent shut-eye every night.

While the quality of my sleep improved dramatically in early sobriety, I soon found myself facing a new challenge: vivid dreams. Before, I never used to dream at all, usually drinking until blackout and then waking up with a startle. Since quitting alcohol, however, I've been having dreams almost every night – some are pleasant, while others are just plain weird. In the initial weeks, I often dreamt that I was drinking wine, but upon waking up, I felt relieved that I was still on track with my sobriety. Yet, I couldn't help but wonder why my own brain seemed to be working against me. It's my brain – you think it would be on my side! Despite the occasional drinking dream, what really troubled me were the nightmares.

I remember having night terrors as a child and the occasional nightmare as an adult, but after quitting alcohol, I began experiencing vivid and terrifying nightmares that resembled horror movies. They were difficult to distinguish from reality and often woke me up with a violent shock, causing me to shiver, shake and even scream on occasion. I'm amazed at the intricate stories my mind can concoct while I sleep, with multiple characters, plot twists and extreme violence that I could never imagine in real life. My nightmares could rival any Steven Spielberg horror film. When we drink heavily, our REM sleep is reduced, but when we stop drinking, our brains rebound and go into overdrive during REM sleep.

It turns out that nightmares are quite common during the first month of alcohol abstinence. There isn't a great deal you can do about this phase, although my ex-partner would disagree – he would recommend that you sleep alone! One night, I woke up to find my partner in bed next to me, and there was a huge spider on his head. It was so big that I was concerned it might be poisonous. I screamed at him to wake up, and in a sleepy haze, he whispered to me, "Go back to sleep." Just at that moment, the spider crawled on to his face. I punched it as hard as I could, and my partner jumped up with a start and started to shout at me:

"What the fuck are you doing?!"

"Saving you from that tarantula, you ungrateful bastard!"

Or at least, I would have done if I were awake and there actually was a spider. It turns out it was just a nightmare hallucination. My partner woke up the next morning irritable and with the beginnings of a black eye. Oops! The moral of the story is, if your partner pisses you off over the next few weeks, you can thump them in the night and blame it on the hallucinations. Mwah ha ha!

Alcohol-free sleep is one of the biggest benefits of sobriety. Once the nightmares subside (and they will!), you will start to sleep like you're dead. I never understood why people say "sleeping like a newborn baby". They only sleep for two hours at a bloody time. Sober sleep is like slipping into an eight-hour coma. Bliss. When you're well rested, everything else is affected for the better – less irritability, improved mood and loads more energy. The list goes on and on. Just thinking about the great sleep I would get that evening was a huge deterrent to picking up a glass. I would tell myself, "Yes, I could drink now, but

I'll only feel good for a really short time, and by three in the morning, I'll massively regret that decision. If I resist, I'll be so happy once I've had eight hours of blissful sleep and wake up with no hangover."

Week three – blood pressure reduces

Ethanol can cause an increase in blood pressure over time. This is because alcohol increases blood levels of the hormone renin, which causes the blood vessels to get smaller in diameter, putting increased pressure on the vessel walls and causing hypertension (high blood pressure). After three weeks of not drinking, your blood pressure will begin to decrease. Lowering your blood pressure can reduce the risk of many other health problems such as strokes and cancers, just to name a few of the major ones.

Week four – liver function improves

In week four, removing alcohol from your body will improve your liver function as the organ starts to rid itself of excess fat. If your liver function is not too severely damaged, it can fully recover. The liver is responsible for over 500 vital processes in your body. The absence of alcohol allows your body to remove contaminants and improve the retention of minerals and vitamins.

Your mood and level of concentration will improve, and irritability will also significantly decrease. The school run, an unfortunate and necessary evil, suddenly doesn't seem quite so sinister!

Alcohol has been shown to negatively affect the proper functioning of the hippocampus, the area of your brain that deals with memory. When you quit drinking, your memory begins to improve. I feel much sharper than I did during my drinking days. I'm also far less forgetful. Some of this is simply not being hungover and living in chaos all the time, but I'm happy to know that my brain has also physically recovered and is firing on all cylinders again.

Weeks four to eight – the boredom phase

Boredom was by far the worst symptom for me, and one of the many reasons why people often conclude that sobriety is boring and go back to drinking at the end of Dry January. After the initial euphoria wore off, I found myself so bored that I could have pulled my own teeth out just for something to do.

Time has always been elusive and scarce for me since I had children. Where does it go? There just aren't enough hours in the day to handle all the tasks of motherhood. But after quitting drinking, I discovered that I had so much time on my hands that I didn't always know what to do with it. Mornings are longer because I wake up earlier, feeling spritely and in a good mood. Sometimes, even now, I still have a moment, a few seconds after waking up, when I remember, Ah, I don't drink, no hangover for me, and I slept nine solid hours! I have become a morning person, and I find the early hours of the day easy to cope with because I feel so much better physically and mentally.

I carried on with the daily grind, cooked dinner, supervised homework, read stories and put my boys to bed. I was okay until I walked downstairs and suddenly found myself alone in the quiet. That was the point when I really struggled during the first couple of months. Not because I was desperate for a drink, but because that's when the boredom would set in. From just after seven in the evening until I went to sleep, I would twiddle my thumbs, watch the clock and replay the old mental images of drunken, wild, fun nights out with friends. The kind of nights when I would declare the next morning, "That was the best weekend ever!" And all of a sudden, I would feel intensely sad, like I was grieving. I looked into the future and the prospect of being sober forever, and I just couldn't imagine it. Forever without wine sounded painful, boring and downright miserable. From seven to eleven every night, I was bored.

In my pink cloud phase, I overlooked the sheer hard work required to maintain sobriety. Changes in circumstances can happen in an instant, which can rattle our emotional state and catapult us back into the danger zone. It's so easy to have a glass of wine because, if you decide to quit, you've given up the one thing you'd normally use to cope. The thing you rely on to survive is the thing that's ruining your life. The epitome of a "catch-22".

I laughed when my eldest, Arthur, sidled up to me one Sunday morning when I was about a month sober. He had a forlorn look on his face and said, "Mummy, what can I do today? I'm so bored!" Without even thinking, I replied with my usual response, "How can you possibly be bored? You have a house full of toys. Go and choose a game. Use your imagination!" The second the words left my mouth, I felt guilty for my blatant hypocrisy. I laughed, because I'd been whining to anyone who would listen about how bored I was, and here I was dismissing my son for complaining about the same thing. In this modern world where there is so much to do, how could he (or I) possibly be bored?

So, how did I deal with boredom, compounded by zero happy hormones?

Firstly, I simply embraced the science and the facts. My brain wasn't making dopamine anymore because it had forgotten how to. I kept reminding myself that it was nothing more than a hormonal imbalance, and it would pass after a couple of months. If I couldn't feel happy, what else could I do to make myself feel better in the meantime? I once had a therapist who explained to me that human beings get happiness from two things: the simple enjoyment of doing something we love, and achievement. Looking at the facts, it suddenly became very clear what I needed to do while in my state of tedium. I couldn't feel happy, but I could be productive. It didn't matter if I felt bored; I could still get things done. I could begin the to-do list that I had perpetually put off from starting. I could get organized. I'll go into this in much more detail later (see How to Quit), as getting my ducks in a row was a crucial part of my recovery.

When you feel bored or unproductive, it's important to start doing something, even if you don't feel like it. Motivation is simply an emotion, the desire to start doing something. I'll cover motivation later, but essentially, if you wait for it, you might end up waiting a long time. The way to get motivated is to start taking action, especially if you don't feel like it. The beauty of motivation is that it's difficult to find, but it almost always materializes after you start taking action.

Here's an idea to start with that works well for me: before you do anything else in the morning, make your bed. This simple act has many mental benefits. It's a short task that helps us concentrate for a few minutes, and it doesn't feel overwhelming. Walking into a room with an unmade bed or getting into an unmade bed to sleep is downright depressing. A freshly made bed has a soothing effect on our minds and can help set our intentions for the day. Before even leaving the bedroom, you've already accomplished one thing. What else can you do in two minutes? If you can make your bed, you can surely handle another small task.

Secondly, we often drink to numb our emotions, but we forget that we have different emotional states because our minds are trying to tell us something. If we feel angry, it's because we feel wronged. If we feel guilty, it's because we think we did something wrong. So why do we feel bored? My interpretation is that the feeling itself isn't negative. It's my mind telling me I'm capable of more because what I'm doing right now isn't fulfilling my emotional needs, which are necessary to make me happy. In the past, I consumed wine to numb any feelings of unfulfillment. But now, my brain is alerting me to the fact that I have four hours every evening with no plans to fill that time. My brain realizes when I'm wasting myself, my time and my life.

Drinking alcohol isn't exciting; it merely numbs the mind to the monotony of boredom, leaving you feeling terrible and wasting your potential. Boredom is your brain's way of telling you that you have untapped potential, and it's up to you to give it direction. Who knows where it could take you? Boredom is the starting point for excitement and accomplishment, and all you need to do is begin.

Alcohol doesn't relieve tedium, engaging in activities does. Think back to what you enjoyed before you started drinking. Personally, I had to revisit my passions from when I was 14 (the last time I was sober): rock music, thrill-seeking, dance, creativity and cooking. Through immersing myself in these activities and discovering new ones, like aerial silks (albeit I frequently end up hanging upside down and tied up in more knots than a hostage victim), I found my true passion in playing guitar. It takes time to fall back in love with life, but it's worth the effort. You just have to be patient with yourself and appreciate the simple things that bring you joy.

Here are some of my favourite simple pleasures: morning coffee; the smell of cakes baking in the oven; cold, crisp, clear blue mornings; the laughter of my children; healthier figures in my bank account; sober sex – OMG – who knew how amazing this is (sorry, Dad)! Finally, the peace and quiet of just sitting with my own thoughts. I didn't think I'd ever be comfortable just sitting in my own company with nothing else going on, but now I love it. It turns out my brain isn't such a scary place, and I actually have a wicked imagination. Now, I spend my "boring" time looking to better my life and the lives of my children.

Remember, in early sobriety, the feeling of monotony is simply your inability to produce dopamine. When it fires up again, you'll know – wait for the orgasm! It's coming!

Weeks four to eight – the grieving phase

I expected to feel a little sad as I envisioned attending live music bars, weddings and parties; where others would be fucked-up on fizz, I would be the quiet, dull one, feeling nothing but jealousy. To avoid this, I planned to side-step large social gatherings and stay away from pubs. However, it didn't work out as I had hoped. Despite avoiding bars during my first hundred days, I still felt a heavy sadness that was intense and akin to grief. It was a longing and aching for the life I had before, and I had not anticipated how monumental giving up alcohol would be. The gaping hole it would leave. This feeling was not dissimilar to the boredom phase; however, it was more of a deep and poignant type of distress.

It wasn't alcohol per se that I was mourning, but the lifestyle that came hand in hand with booze and laughter. It doesn't take long after quitting to start romanticizing memories of the good times, the great nights out, and the stories that result in raucous belly laughing with friends. All I could think about was what I believed I was missing. Much like when we grieve the loss of a person, we focus on all the good times and forget the bad. Undeniably, I have had some great nights out after drinking a lot of wine. I have funny stories spanning 25 years that, when told now, still bring a smile to my face. We romanticize the past and look for the good stuff, but it doesn't change the fact that there was a really bad side too. For every fun time, every laugh, every fond memory, there is a trade-off – stupid decisions, broken relationships, ruined friendships, injuries, embarrassment, disturbed sleep, anxiety, depression, health issues, financial issues, lost employment, guilt, violence and shame. Just remember this: if an absolute arsehole dies, nobody talks shit about them at the funeral. But that doesn't change the fact that they were still an arsehole. Alcohol is exactly the same. Like a domestic violence perpetrator who beats their partner black and blue, then buys a gift to apologize and showers their victim in compliments and affection, the good doesn't even come close to outweighing the bad. So overall, it's just never going to be worth it. Remember the good times with fondness, but don't forget the bad – they are the reason why you want to quit in the first place, and I imagine, the very reason you're reading this book.

Week four and beyond – the "who am I?" phase

This one I didn't expect. The "who am I?" phase is akin to a mid-life crisis. As it happened, my divorce was granted during my sober journey, and I turned 40 in the same year – so maybe there was a little panic about ageing mixed in with my newfound sobriety. Either way, this was a significant phase for me. I started drinking when I was 14 so I had literally never been an adult who didn't drink, aside from during pregnancy. What I didn't realize is that meant I had no idea who I actually was. I was a stranger to myself. Drunk me was outgoing, loud, confident and sexy. At least that's what I thought. Looking back at some of the cringeworthy things I've said and done over two-plus decades, I was brash, obnoxious, arrogant and whatever the opposite of sexy is. My life, my personality and my self-perception have all been an illusion. I have lived my whole adult existence through an ethanol filter. I've lost hundreds of hours of time in blackouts. I've lost even more time in a fuzzy delirium. I've lost countless mornings to hangovers. I had absolutely no idea who I was as a person.

In the first few weeks, this discovery was very unsettling. It was like listening to a new voice in my head. It sounded like me, but I'd never heard someone talking in that way before – a way that was exempt from chaos, drama and trouble. Now I've learned that I really enjoy my own company I've realized that I used alcohol to become extroverted in spite of myself. I no longer need to constantly be around people in order to stay out of my head and ensure I'm perpetually distracted. When my children are asleep, I don't have to drown out the incessant negative internal chatter, because it doesn't exist anymore. I don't need to silence the voice that berates and ridicules me. The voice that tells me I'm a terrible person who doesn't deserve happiness. Now I'm starting to get used to this new voice. The one that is proud of my sober life. The one that is grateful for my dedication to my children. The one that tells me I am good enough and I can achieve great things. I may not know you personally, but if you're asking "who am I?", what I can tell you is that the sober version of you is better. Smarter. Nicer. Sexier. Happier. Braver. Healthier. Kinder. Think of quitting alcohol as the removal of your evil twin – your good side is only just getting started. Now is the time to find out who you are and what you are truly capable of.

Two months and beyond – the zen phase

This is the phase I hoped for, longed for even. At the very beginning of my journey, I started keeping a journal. I had one relapse after the first five days. When I picked up a bottle of red, I decided to write down how I felt after every glass. It was surprising that when I paid attention and concentrated on the actual feelings and thoughts going through my mind, they weren't actually positive. This is an extract from that journal entry:

Five days sober and opened the wine – because it's there, I'm home alone and I'm bored… tastes terrible. No feeling of relief. Just guilt. Second glass – feel disgusting. Tastes awful. Feel sick. Disappointed with myself. Slightly numbing sensation but it doesn't even feel like a benefit.

I don't remember writing this next line… It was the last thing I wrote. I've never touched a drop since.

One bottle down. I feel sick, sad and generally discontent. This does not feel good.

Whenever I felt like I wanted a glass of wine, I reread that last line – a reminder that after one bottle, I will not feel better.

I will not feel good. At the time I wrote that journal entry and for all the entries before that, I documented my anxiety levels each day, and I now get all of my clients to do the same. When I was drinking, my anxiety levels were always nine or ten out of ten, and some days I'd even score myself an 11 out of ten – just to acknowledge how extremely stressed I felt. Within seven days of being sober, my anxiety levels reduced significantly. Now, they are rarely higher than three out of ten, and consistently low. I've not had a period of sustained calm like this since I was a teenager. It begs the question, have my last 25 years of anxiety been caused by alcohol? Quite possibly, I think. All I know is that since I've quit drinking, I've felt a whole lot less stressed. No heart racing, palpitations, constant worry, fretting about my health, catastrophizing or a general sense of panic. After a lifetime of anxiety, the absence of this feeling is hard to believe. It's like walking around in a bit of a bubble, in some sort of parallel universe where extreme stress can't reach me anymore. I react better to problems. I keep things in proportion. I feel zen!

The absolute best stage of quitting is getting to the two-month mark. When your dopamine levels begin to spark back up again, your energy returns with it. This feeling is nothing short of incredible. For me, it was like someone literally injected life back into me. The exhaustion ebbed away and I started to regain a real desire for life – an appetite for fun!

So far, I've only mentioned the physical and mental benefits. But there is a whole other category of improvement when it comes to social connection: relationships with other people. Firstly, and most importantly, my relationship with my children has become much stronger and closer since I became sober. I always felt like I was a good mum, even when I was drinking, but there were so many ways in which I wasn't fully present or showing up for them like I am now. I would count down the minutes until my children went to bed, so I could sit and drink my Pinot in peace. I would rush through the bedtime routine. I would wake up hungover and irritable. I didn't play as much. I didn't listen properly. Mentally, I was in such a bad place that I was never really happy. I lived in my head, always worrying. My brain was just elsewhere. Now I love the bedtime routine. It's quality time spent chatting with my boys, getting to know what random, wonderful little people they're growing up to be. I listen – really listen. We read together. I play. I'm far less quick to anger. Yes – I still get irritable. Of course I do. I'm a mum. "Mumming" is fucking tough! Giving up alcohol is amazing, but it's not a miracle cure. When my boys fight with each other, I still sometimes fantasize about launching them down the stairs. I'm human. Nonetheless, I'm far calmer in general, and the intensity of love that I feel for my children is now reflected in the way I treat them, and in the way I treat myself.

The zen stage is beyond epic! The reward for all of your hard work. When your brain synapses begin to fire up and flood your body with natural happy hormones. In the beginning, this phase can appear completely elusive. There were moments when I didn't believe I would get there. Maybe this stage will never arrive for me. Maybe I am different. An anomaly. If you take nothing else away from this chapter – remember this – EVERYONE gets to this stage. It's as certain as gravity.

Think about it. When you drink, and you keep going, you know what will happen. You will eventually black out. The hangover symptoms are entirely predictable. Surely then, common sense dictates that the reversal, quitting alcohol, must also have an inevitable list of symptoms. If drinking makes you feel like shit, stopping drinking will eventually feel good.

Getting through the first three months is not simple if you don't understand what is happening in your body. But now you're aware of the stages, it is simple. It's not easy at times, granted, but it is straightforward. There is a beautiful safety in knowing that there is a structure to quitting. There is a timeline. And it has an end. A fucking awesome one.

One Random Hot Day in July 2006

> "Insanity is doing the same thing over and over again and expecting different results."

Anonymous

I love summer, and I used to very much look forward to the warmer months when I was a drinker. Sitting in a pub garden for hours on end was a regular pastime of mine. As much as I loved wasting the day away in a drunken haze, there were inherent problems caused by boozy sessions in the sun. I would start drinking sooner, get drunk quicker and feel much worse the next day. I have no doubt that severe dehydration was a factor. I rarely drank water, and most days, I would get sunburned because I was too fucked-up to care about sunscreen. I have had more day-long drinking sessions than I care to remember, but there are a few memories that are so disturbing that even the passage of time has not lessened the detail of my recollection. I don't recall much about significant events like my first day at school or many of my younger childhood birthdays, but I have shockingly clear images of the times where I really fucked up after drinking too much.

Now that I am sober, I can look at these stories and tell them with some humour, largely because they are no longer a threat. When I was drinking, these stories would beat me around the head during the night in a series of mental blows, fuelling the already crippling anxiety caused by the comedown of a heavy session. They were the basis of insipid self-hatred and a constant worrying reminder of the risks I was taking every time I popped the cork of a wine bottle. When I drank, I was dangerous, and anything could happen.

When I was 24 years old, I spent one particularly gloriously hot Saturday in a pub garden in the middle of a lovely housing estate in Fleet. It was a new development of beautiful townhouses, and a friend of mine, Louisa, had recently moved there with her boyfriend. She had invited me to have lunch at her new local pub and to stay for the night, so I could drink and not have to drive back home.

I always started a drinking session with a large Pinot Grigio with ice. I liked it super cold so I could drink it faster, wanting to feel numb to every negative emotion as soon as possible. My aim was always to get fucked-up, which is crazy considering the risky consequences of doing so. I often made a fool of myself and suffered from horrendous anxiety before social occasions. To turn off that feeling, I would get drunk as quickly as possible, caring a lot less about being a dickhead when I was plastered.

My memory of that day is patchy at best. I chatted up countless strangers, and for the life of me, I can't remember what we talked about. My poison of choice was usually wine (I wasn't a big fan of spirits). I could always tell when I was about to hit my limit and end up hugging the toilet, which is precisely why I avoided hard liquor like the plague. But after a couple of bottles of wine, my standards went out the window, and everything sounded like a fantastic idea. So, when the kind strangers offered me shots of sambuca, I downed them without hesitation. My drunk brain thought it was a stroke of genius!

Louisa's partner could see that I was a mess and suggested getting food before going home. We went to the local pizza place and then back to the house. I crawled up the stairs on my hands and knees, desperate to get to bed and sleep it off. I went to close the bedroom door, but Louisa pushed it open and handed me a two-pence coin.

"The dog can open doors with her paws. You need to close the door and use this coin to lock yourself in by doing this." Louisa demonstrated, placing the coin into a brass notch under the door handle. She slid the coin into the groove and turned it to lock the door. "Got it?!" she asked.

"Yeeeesh," I slurred. I closed the door and tried to lock it, but I was so hammered that I had lost most of my fine motor skills. It took several attempts before I could get the coin to find the groove, but I eventually managed to lock the door. It was stifling in the room, the height of summer. I opened the window and stripped off naked, still feeling too hot. I didn't care and lay down in the bed, instantly slipping into a drunken coma.

Like clockwork, I woke up in the middle of the night, probably around three, which was the usual witching hour. I needed to pee and was dying of thirst, but I hadn't got myself a glass of water before bed, as I would normally in my own home. I woke up disoriented, not knowing where I was, and it was pitch-black dark, so I couldn't see a fucking thing.

I crawled out of bed and felt for the walls. Okay. So far so good. I felt along to get to the door. Nope. No door here. I felt some more. Still no door. I started to panic. I couldn't find a light switch. I couldn't find the door. And I was about to wet myself. I could feel the panic surge in my chest. My search for the door became frantic. I knew I wasn't at home. But where was I? Who cares. Wherever I was, there had to be a bloody door! I finally found a handle and pulled hard. I walked through the door, but was met by a wall. What the fuck! How is there a door behind the door?! I pushed. It wasn't solid. Something must have been stuck behind the door. I pushed harder. And harder. Finally, a crack! The wall gave way. Oh shit. I suddenly realized that I wasn't pushing on a door. I was inside a wardrobe. And I'd just ripped the back off it – clean off. In case you're wondering, I did not find Narnia.

I climbed out of the wardrobe and instantly remembered where I was. I found the light switch, fumbled around with the coin and managed to get out. I ran to the bathroom. I grabbed the handle, so relieved that I was about to get to the toilet, but I couldn't open it. It was locked. Unbeknown to me at that time, Louisa had also locked this door with a coin. And I had no idea where I'd put the bloody two-pence piece. Fuck!

The only other toilet in the house was in the en suite to Louisa's bedroom – where she was sleeping with her beau. I couldn't go in there. I was naked! I ran as fast as I could down the stairs. I turned the key to the patio doors that led to the garden, staggered outside and squatted on the lawn. I didn't care that I was naked and the garden was overlooked. I was just super relieved I hadn't pissed myself. Hopefully everyone would be asleep anyway. Crisis averted! As I squatted in the garden, the dog, a huge Alsatian, sat in front of me and cocked his head, staring right at me. I really felt like he was judging me in that moment.

"This is your fault! If it wasn't for you the door wouldn't have been locked!" I cussed out loud.

I scuttled back to bed and closed the door behind me. I didn't lock it. I wasn't going through that again. I managed to drift back off to sleep. I've no clue how long I was asleep for, but at some point, I started to dream about vomiting. I woke up with a jolt and in a split second, I realized I was dreaming about being sick, because I felt sick. Before I could even get to my feet, I threw up everywhere. And I mean everywhere. Over myself, the bed, Louisa's partner's suit (which was hanging over the end of the bedstead), my clothes (which were also on the bed), the walls and the carpet. Did I mention this was a brand-new house?

I knew I was going to vomit again, and I needed the bathroom. I couldn't do this in the garden. I ran to the bathroom (having found that bloody coin) – naked, covered in vomit and using one hand to stop it from running down my body. It didn't work. I left a trail of vomit along the carpet from the bedroom to the bathroom. I managed to get the door open and slid the vomit into the sink before violently throwing up in the toilet. Once I'd finished, my stomach pulsated in pain and I sat on the bathroom floor waiting for the intensity of the cramping to pass.

I felt like absolute death but I knew I needed to clean up. I washed myself in the sink using hand soap and dragged myself back to the bedroom. I stripped the bed, and took the pile of vomit-soaked laundry downstairs, which I stuffed into the washing machine – save for the duvet and the suit – which I had to put in the boot of my car later that morning to take to the dry cleaners. I searched the cupboards for cleaning stuff and crept back up the stairs. Naked, on my hands and knees, I started to scrub the carpet, quietly praying that Louisa and her boyfriend wouldn't wake up. In this moment, naked and on my knees with a scouring pad in hand, I vowed I would never drink again. I've lost count of the amount of "I'll never drink again" moments I've had in this life. I felt total shame. How could I have got into such a state? Why didn't I stop drinking earlier? Why did I do those fucking shots!

After the clean-up mission, I crawled back into the unmade bed and went back to sleep. I was so exhausted from being sick that I drifted right back off into a comatose sleep. When I woke in the morning, my head felt like it was full of lead. I could feel the acid swilling around in my stomach. I still felt horrifically sick, but there was nothing left in my body to bring up.

When Louisa woke up, I was painfully apologetic. I promised to get the duvet and the suit cleaned and bring them back. She was understanding and sympathetic. Way more than I deserved.

I'd love to say that this awful experience was the catalyst for a period of abstinence. But once the shame began to wear off, the laundry was cleaned and I felt like "normal" again – I was straight back to the wine. I told myself I could moderate. That I wouldn't do shots. Yes. That was the problem. If only I had stopped at wine, I would never have got in that mess. Wine isn't the problem. Neither am I. It was the sambuca that fucked me up. As long as I avoid that, I'll be fine.

This was a cycle I remained in for many, many years. Drink to excess. Do something regrettable. Feel the shame. Justify. Move on. Repeat.

Now I'm sober, these memories aren't harrowing at all. They're actually a beautiful reminder of how free I am. I will never again have to worry when I socialize – because drinking orange juice will, quite simply, not turn me into a dickhead.

Major Life Events and Trauma

> *"You have within you, right now, everything you need to deal with whatever the world can throw at you."*
>
> Brian Tracy

Major life events and trauma. Ugh!

Sobriety can make so many areas of your life improve for the better, but the one thing it can't do is erase major or traumatic events from your life. They're inevitable. However great life can be, there will always be difficult times.

In 1999, Baz Luhrmann released a song called "Everybody's Free to Wear Sunscreen". If you haven't heard it before, have a listen. It's beautiful and highly profound. One of the lines in the song talks about how the things in life that really cause us troubles are not the things that we worry about – they're the things that side-swipe you unexpectedly on a Tuesday. Ironically, it was one of my mum's favourites. Ironic, because on some idle Tuesday morning (Tuesday 17 March 2020, to be precise), I was blindsided with a call that my worried mind could never have imagined.

I was working at the office when my mobile unexpectedly rang at about ten in the morning. My dad. He was crying.

"Your mum fell when she was running. She banged her head. She's in hospital. They think she has a bleed on the brain. Can you come home?"

I tried to calm my dad down. I was sure he was overreacting. He does that. When someone is really sick, like when my nanna was about to die, he called me and described her as "very poorly". When my mum fell and broke her arm one time, he called me to say there had been a "terrible accident". When my dad was calm, things were bad. When he was frantic, everything was generally okay. He was frantic. She would be fine.

I nonetheless quickly went home, packed a few things and my then husband and I got in the car to drive to my home town of Chester, in the north-west of England. I suddenly had a thought that made me panic. Did my mum fall and then hit her head, or did she hit her head because she fell – because something more sinister was going on? I felt my body flood with anxiety. The soul-crushing kind.

About an hour into my journey, somewhere on the M40, I got a call from my dad, saying, "Your mum is really poorly. They're doing some tests. They don't know what happened yet, but her blood pressure is really low."

Shit. If she was "really poorly", in Dad's language, that meant "about to die". I could feel it. I sat in silence and prayed. I still don't know if I believe in God. I believe in "something" spiritual going on in the universe. But at that point, I wanted to hedge my bets, so I silently begged God to make sure my mum was okay. I don't remember much else about that car journey. It was like I was having an out-of-body experience. There but not there. The phone rang again. My dad. Screaming.

"She's gone! She's gone! I've lost her! I've lost her."

I couldn't breathe. My sister, Steph, was at the hospital with my dad when he called me. He was in a room with a closed door. Steph has told me she will forever be haunted by the sounds of my screaming. So loud she could hear me through the phone and that closed door. Pure, unadulterated pain.

I have no memory of the day after this point. I couldn't see my mum at the hospital. It was right at the beginning of the pandemic. She had already been taken to the morgue when I arrived. They needed the bed.

We would later discover that my mum had died of an aortic dissection. A condition I'd never even heard of before. A heart valve effectively explodes. The mortality rate is 99 per cent. She didn't have a chance. There were no symptoms and no warning signs. It was her sixty-second birthday the day before. Our last conversation had been lovely and she'd thanked me for a Michelin-star restaurant voucher I'd bought her, but she would never get to enjoy.

The suddenness of my mum's death felt violent. I hadn't felt emotional pain like that before. All I knew was that I wanted to block it out. Luckily, so did the rest of my family. I can't remember much at all from that week I spent at my family home. Partly because I was traumatized, but mostly because I was drunk – constantly. We all were. At the time my mum died, I would generally drink every other day. I instantly started drinking daily, and my tolerance very quickly increased. After I lost my mum, I drank a bottle of wine at a minimum, every single night.

Just like that. I went from some degree of moderation to a daily drinker. I didn't want to drink. I didn't want to get drunk. I just wanted to shut out the pain as best as I could. And I wasn't the only one.

My dad was a creature of habit and had always been particularly strict with his own intake of alcohol. He committed to never drinking from Sunday to Thursday and would consume a single bottle of red wine on a Friday and Saturday night. He did this for years. When my mum died, he went from two bottles of wine a week to three bottles of wine a day. Instantly. Yes, you read that right. Steph and I didn't believe he would survive that first year. We didn't believe he would be with us for the first Christmas without my mum. He was totally broken. Forty-two years of marriage. And she was gone.

For a year and a half my dad drank three bottles of wine a day. He eventually stopped when I quit, and he started to read my blogs. I didn't know how much he was drinking until he confessed, after he stopped. I asked him why he drank so much.

"I just wanted to sleep. I was in too much pain to sleep."

Pain. The reason everyone drinks. Sudden increase in pain – sudden increase in drinking. This, right here, is why moderation can be so dangerous. You never know when you'll be blindsided on some idle Tuesday morning.

Unbeknown to me, the death of my mum was the catalyst for my journey to sobriety. It kick-started a downward spiral, and once I reached close to the bottom, I was then able to quit. I sometimes wonder what would have happened if my mum hadn't died. I honestly believe I would still be drinking. The only reason I stopped was that I got to a place where I had battered my body so much that I was really fed up of feeling like shit all the time. If my mum were still alive, I don't think I would have entered that period of total self-destruction, and eventually, reinvention.

After I became sober, I often wondered if the death of someone else close to me would cause me to relapse. I couldn't imagine being able to cope with such a huge life event without the use of alcohol. The ability to numb the pain, even temporarily, was all I could do to cope with my mum's death in the early days. How do you even begin to deal with that level of sadness without some chemical help? Unfortunately, I didn't have to wait long to find out.

On an otherwise uneventful Christmas Eve, I was scrolling through my Facebook feed when I saw a photo of Sara, my dear friend whom I'd met some 20 years earlier. It was a professional-looking photo – not uncommon. I always saw videos and photos of Sara on my feed. She had single-handedly set up her own property empire in Florida, where she lived with her husband and three-year-old daughter. I often saw videos of Sara showing off her latest project – usually a beautiful, palatial home she had renovated and would then sell. She was made for being on camera and had previously worked on home shopping television channels selling jewellery. Much like the gems she sold, she sparkled.

This photo looked different though. It looked like a news article. Strange. Maybe she was promoting her business through the media? Then I read the headline.

"British real estate agent, forty, shot dead in Florida."

I couldn't breathe. I must have read it wrong. I read the headline over and over. I could not process what I was seeing. My friend. Dead? Murdered?! How could that be possible?

Sara was shot the day before, on 23 December 2021, in a case of mistaken identity. Her murderer believed her to be someone else with whom he'd had a grievance. He shot her while she was sitting in her car, and she died shortly after. Just like that. My beautiful friend. Twenty years of friendship. I was beyond devastated. I was also sober. Just five weeks.

I thought about drinking. But something stopped me. I knew I would feel worse. I knew it wouldn't help. Alcohol couldn't bring her back. It might shut off my feelings for a while, but I'd inevitably feel ten times worse the next day. So, I cried. I cried more than I'd cried in years. Much more than when my mum died. Not because I cared less for my mum, but because I actually allowed myself to feel the sadness. I sat with it. It wasn't pretty. It was excruciatingly painful. I grieved.

Sitting with painful feelings is tough, but what I found was that I recovered from grief in a completely different way – it was tolerable, and it was much quicker – because I allowed myself to process those difficult emotions. I will always feel a deep sadness when I think of Sara and of the experiences I will never get to share with her. I still sometimes cry tears for her darling daughter, who will grow up without the most amazing mother she could have ever wished for. But I also have a sense of peace. An internal calmness that I didn't have when I was drinking. I know I can deal with tough experiences – as long as I am sober. I will cope.

I lost my mother and a dear friend in relatively quick succession. Before these awful events, I was terrified of death. When I was five years old, I remember being obsessed with mortality. My mum had to buy me a book about it just to try to help me process my fears – it didn't work. I spent my childhood and most of my adult life fearing the inevitable. After Sara died, something shifted. I chose to think about dying. Yes, I know, I sound very morbid – but the inescapable truth is that we will all die one day.

Losing two people so significant in my life has been really tough. I don't think it's something you ever get over – but time, as with all other things, makes it easier. The biggest lesson I've learned through these experiences is that life is short and extraordinarily precious. Sobriety has massively opened my eyes to this fact. I can't believe the time I have wasted in oblivion. The time I've wasted making terrible choices. The time I've wasted hungover. Time is the most precious commodity we have. I treated time like it was abundant and infinite – it's not.

Now when I think about death, it doesn't scare me. It inspires me. I'm motivated to use the time I have, to enjoy it as much as possible, to see the people I love and hold them close, and tell them how much I love them – because who knows when it will be our last encounter.

What I now find really terrifying is the prospect of not fulfilling my potential. Not making the most of the little time I have on this planet. None of us knows how much time we have – every day is so incredibly valuable. When we choose to think about death, it reminds us to really live life. That we don't have endless time or opportunity. Only now. What do you want from your life? What creates a spark for you? Find out and go for it! Don't wait. Don't think, Ah, I'll get round to it one day. Remind yourself that one day, this beautiful life will all be over, so cherish your time and make the most of it while you can. What can you achieve sober? The sky really is the limit.

Alcohol Gives You Confidence, Right?

> "You gain strength, courage and confidence by every experience in which you really stop to look fear in the face... You must do the thing you think you cannot do."
>
> Eleanor Roosevelt

This next story will haunt me to my grave. Usually, I tell it for one reason only – to make people laugh. After the last chapter, I think you need a giggle. I'm a big believer that if you have suffered any kind of misfortune, but there is comedy in it, at least you can get some good from the experience by making others chuckle. I've always loved the idea of being a stand-up comedian. Standing on a stage, telling your story, and making a roomful of people laugh in unison, must be one of the biggest natural highs a person can get, though I'm not sure I'd ever have the confidence to actually get up there and do it.

Self-confidence is a tough thing to come by, which is one of the many reasons we turn to alcohol for "Dutch courage". I've used alcohol in many situations to give myself that mythical "boost" – karaoke, wedding speeches, and I once had a large glass of Pinot during a telephone interview for a job to "calm" my nerves. But these are child's play examples compared to this story. I took "Dutch courage" to a new level. And it wasn't pretty.

When I was 18 years old, I was living in London and studying law at Kingston University. Towards the back end of my first year, I was running seriously low on money. I had zero idea of how to budget, I'd spent my student loan in its entirety (mostly on clothes and getting battered), and my bank account was running on fumes. I was heading back to Chester after the term had ended, and, the night before my trip, I was due to meet friends at the local Wetherspoons in Surbiton. For those of you not from the UK, Wetherspoons is a chain of bars that sells cheap alcohol from early in the morning. These pubs are renowned for being the stomping ground of students – and alcoholics who need to start drinking before breakfast.

I was running late, but I needed to get some cash out in case my friends were doing a kitty, so I ran to the ATM machine next to the pub. I was mortified to discover I was down to my last £10. I withdrew the remainder of the money in my account and ran straight to the pub to meet my friends. Everyone was already sitting down with their first drinks – so I went to the bar. When I went to pay for my first drink, my purse was empty. I slowly filled with panic as I remembered that in my rush, I'd left the £10 note in the machine. I ran back to the ATM, but as suspected, someone had taken it. I was gutted! Luckily, I had decent friends who were prepared to buy my drinks for the night, but it sparked a conversation about the serious lack of cash flow we were dealing with as students. I moaned about how expensive it was to live in the south, especially London, having been raised in the north of England, where it is monumentally cheaper.

"Yeah, but you're lucky. You're hot. You could just go and work in a strip club," one of the guys piped up.

I laughed it off, of course. But the suggestion niggled away in the back of my mind for the next week. Was this genuinely a quick way to make money fast? Could I do it? I remembered an advert I had seen in a newspaper called *The Stage*, which I used to buy when I was 15 years old. It contained various adverts for music auditions, and I bought it because I was convinced there would one day be an opportunity that would propel me to fame – I basically wanted to be a Spice Girl. Needless to say, such an advert never arose, but I remembered seeing one for an infamous strip club in Soho, London. They were advertising for dancers and in the job description it said "No grooming required". I vividly remember turning to one of my school friends, laughing, and saying, "That sounds like a dog parlour!"

The memory of the advert continued to play on my mind over the summer holidays. This was in the year 2000, and I didn't own a laptop. I had barely discovered the internet, so when I returned to university, I did what everyone did back then: I picked up the *Yellow Pages*. Sure enough, the club was still standing. I was terrified, but the prospect of making loads of money was enough to give me the courage to pick up the phone. I don't remember anything about that conversation other than one line, "Auditions are on Tuesdays at eight p.m. See you then."

Gulp! I took the train from Surbiton to Waterloo and then hopped on the London Underground to get to Soho. I felt absolutely sick to my stomach and utterly terrified. I knocked on the front door to the club. A beautiful 20-something-year-old lady with long dark hair asked if I was there for the audition. I nodded silently and was ushered downstairs into a long changing room. There was a U-shape of dressing tables, and each space had its own mirror, surrounded by bulbs. It looked like every picture I had ever seen of an actress's dressing room in the movies. Only this one was for strippers, obviously.

"Stand there. Take your clothes off. Leave your underwear on. I'll get Pete," she said.

I duly obliged. It was cold and my body was covered in goosebumps. I stood alone in the dressing room and looked down. I was wearing an old white bra that was now a distinct shade of grey. And purple knickers with flowers on. Shit. Why didn't I see this coming?!

Unbeknown to me at that time, Pete was the club owner. I've no idea how old he was, but when he walked into the room, my first guess was about 70. He looked me up and down.

"You can start tomorrow. You're going to need matching underwear."

Yeah. I figured.

Pete turned on his heel and left the room. The beautiful dark-haired lady came back in.

"Okay. You're going to need matching underwear and a suspender belt. Bring a nice dress. Come here early tomorrow so you can meet the house mother and she can talk you through everything. Be here at seven."

I nodded again, then swiftly took the train back home. And that was it. I had a job – no experience necessary. I had never stripped before, had no idea what to do – I was a completely naive 18-year-old girl who was about to enter the underworld of Soho – what could possibly go wrong?!

First things first, I needed matching underwear. Now, where do I get that? I didn't own any. I was single, had never really been in an adult relationship, and matching underwear was certainly not something that had ever been considered by my 18-year-old brain. The only underwear shopping I'd ever witnessed was when my mum had bought her bras from Marks & Spencer. Guess I'll start there then.

I went to Marks & Spencer in Kingston and headed for the underwear selection. I opted for a black lace set – I figured I couldn't go far wrong with black. I remember that it cost a small fortune for me, and I just hoped I would earn enough to compensate myself and pay back the credit card I had just used for the first time. Tomorrow, I'd be wearing this in public. And more importantly, taking it off. I shuddered.

I don't remember much about the journey to the strip club on that first night, but I recall every detail once I walked through the doors of that infamous building. The same beautiful dark-haired lady was there, and she told me to meet the house mother in the dressing room. I walked down the dark staircase. There were black-and-white pictures of stunning naked women adorning the walls. Wow, I do not look anything like these women. I was a girl, not long out of high school, and I had only just discovered that matching underwear was a "thing".

"DARLING!"

The house mother came striding up to me and grabbed me by the hand. She was a large, buxom woman – sturdy, bold and with such an air of confidence about her, she looked like she belonged on a stage herself. Maybe not at a strip club, but Broadway, absolutely.

"Follow me, darling. I have to get through this quickly before the club opens. Have you danced before?"

"Er, no."

"Have you been in a club before?"

"Nope."

"Do you have any idea how this works?"

"Not a clue." I was starting to sweat.

"Oh Lord. Okay. This is how it works. Twenty pounds a dance, honey. You dance on the stage there. Your aim is to get the men to sit at a table. That's where they spend the money. They have to buy a bottle of champagne at minimum. They pay you eighty pounds to sit for an hour with them at the table. This includes two dances. They can buy extra."

I looked around at the club. It was really dark and smaller than I had thought it would be inside – no more than 15 tables and a stage with a single pole at the back.

"They don't just give you money. You have to hustle, baby girl. Talk them into it. You can buy your own drinks. The men can buy you drinks. DO NOT get drunk. Got it?"

"Got it." I started to feel hotter. I wanted to start drinking now. There wasn't a chance in hell I was getting up on that stage without some Dutch courage. I was already a pretty heavy social drinker. I didn't drink every night, but when I did, I got drunk. Every. Single. Time. Still, I thought, I'll be fine. I'll be too busy making money anyway.

"Now don't worry, darling. The other girls will show you how to dance. The pole isn't used much. It's stage dancing here, okay?"

"Okay." Now what the fuck is stage dancing?! It's fine. I'll just watch and copy. How hard can it be?

The house mother ushered me back down from the club and into the dressing room.

"Now get dressed and put your make-up on so I can get a look at you before you go into the club. You'll need a garter. You can pay me back when you've had your first dance."

The house mother demonstrated how to wrap money around the garter and secure it so it was safe with an elastic band. Excellent. I had all the kit I needed!

Now the instruction I was previously given was not very specific. "Bring a nice dress." I only had one nice dress. I wore it for my high school prom. It was long and made of black and silver lace. Very pretty. As I started to change, the other girls started to flood into the room. As I watched the roomful of stunning women get changed, I wasn't entirely sure my dress was the right choice for a stripper. They were all wearing short dresses. Not to worry. It's a minor detail. I still look okay.

As I finished applying my make-up, I went to see to the house mother for her approval, before I was released into the wild.

"DARLING! You'll look like a goddam ghost on that stage! Stage lighting, remember! Make-up! Get in make-up! Quickly!"

I was gently pushed into a small room where two men were sitting, armed with brushes and more make-up than I'd ever seen in my life. I sat in front of a lighted mirror and they started to apply layer upon layer of foundation to my face. I'd never really worn make-up before. I used a minimal amount and didn't really know what the hell I was doing with it – these were the days before YouTube tutorials. By the time I was finished in that chair, I was unrecognizable. Under normal lighting, I looked like an absolute horror show. I was so heavily made up I couldn't see my own skin. Still, I'll look better when I get on stage. The stage. OMG. I really needed a drink.

The house mother led me back into the club.

"It won't be long before we open. Get ready!"

Get ready? By doing what exactly? How on earth do you "get ready" for something like this? Wine. That's how. I ordered a glass of Pinot Grigio from the bar and sank half the glass in a few gulps. I felt better. Well, not better, but I started to care a little less than I did a few moments before. A couple of girls walked up to me. They were stunningly beautiful and both about 20 years old, a blonde and a brunette.

They were dressed much more appropriately than I was, in short, slinky dresses and humongous Perspex heels, while I was wearing black stilettos with mid-sized heels. Mmm, I definitely need new shoes for next time.

The brunette asked, "First night?"

"Yes, I'm shitting myself. I've never danced, I don't know what to do," I replied.

"Don't worry!" the blonde girl said. "When you get your first dance, we'll come on stage with you. Just watch and copy. You don't have to take your knickers off until right at the last second before the end of the song. Then we leave the stage."

"Got it. Thank you so much!" I replied, realizing that I had forgotten about the fact I would need to remove my underwear.

The doors opened, and the first men walked in. A tall blond man made a beeline for me. "This is your first night?" he asked in an Australian accent.

"Oh shit! Is it that obvious? How did you know?" I asked.

"Well, you're not dressed like the others, you're not wearing stripper shoes, and you look terrified," he replied with a chuckle.

Oh, for fuck's sake. I felt the effects of the wine rapidly wearing off, and the anxiety began to feel like a crushing sensation in my chest.

"Would you like some champagne?" the man asked.

"Yes!" I replied, maybe a little too enthusiastically.

"Okay, well, I'll get a bottle, and we can sit at a table," he said.

"Okay. I think I'm supposed to charge you eighty pounds for that," I said.

"That's fine," he said, smiling and handed me £80 in cash. I folded it and wrapped it around my garter, as per the lesson I'd had 20 minutes ago. Okay. So, I'm doing this! I was the first girl to sit at a table that night. The man later told me he chose me because I was new. I wasn't a "hustler" yet. It was endearing, apparently.

I drank the bubbles and felt relieved to be sitting with a man who was actually very pleasant. We talked about life in general, and after an hour or so of chatting, he ordered bottle number two of some ridiculously overpriced champagne.

"You don't have to dance for me if you don't want to, but if you're going to work here, then you're going to have to get up there at some point. Maybe you should get it over and done with. Don't worry, I won't laugh. I'll be supportive," he said.

This was the nicest possible scenario for my first night and first dance. A man who didn't put pressure on me and was clearly feeling how nervous I was. He was absolutely right, of course. I needed to get up there.

"Okay. I'm doing it!" I declared, feeling pretty drunk after having half a bottle of champagne and a large glass of Pinot. I walked up to Blonde and Brunette and asked if they would come up with me. Not one girl had danced yet. We were the first of the night.

The girls escorted me up the stairs to the stage, and we waited in the wings for the song to start. I couldn't tell you what it was. Partly because I was wasted, but also because I was in sheer panic, and all I could focus on was the stage.

As the song began, Blonde and Brunette elegantly waltzed up to the front of the stage and began writhing around. I did my best to copy. I felt okay. I didn't feel like I was doing anything totally out of place. That was, until they took their dresses off.

One flick of the wrist, slide the dress overhead and toss. It looked simple enough. Ah, I was wearing my long prom dress. Oh, and did I forget to tell you, it was fitted… and tight.

I grabbed the dress from the middle and tried to slide it up as naturally as I could, but the fabric gathered at the top. I quickly grabbed the bottom of the dress and tried to hike it up, to push the middle along – a little like when you're trying to put on a pair of tights. I managed to get the material all bunched in the middle, and the only way to get it off was to cross my arms and pull it overhead, like you would with a sweater. It didn't work. It was jammed tight. I got stuck with half of the dress over my head, frantically tugging the fabric to pull the rest over. I could feel the sweat pouring down my body. It took the best part of 20 seconds to get unstuck. Frantic tugging, sweating and some more tugging. I must have looked like a crazy person trying to escape from a straitjacket.

When I finally got it off, I could see the Australian had his hand placed strategically over his mouth. He was smiling and trying his best to hide it. I couldn't see anyone else. With the stage lights, it was so dark in the audience that only the front row was visible. But I could see a lot of shoulders. In my drunken haze, what I had failed to realize was that the club was now full.

Dress on the floor, I mentally pushed on. No drama. Next time, I'll know not to wear a tight dress. I can still do this! I glanced down at my matching M&S underwear. Pretty sexy, if I don't say so myself! Blonde and Brunette whipped off their bras in a swift motion. I didn't manage quite such finesse, but I got it off with less of a fight than the dress. So, I'm topless in public. Not as bad as I thought! I couldn't see any faces. I won't see these people again. Who cares?! I've got good boobs! I'm making money having a little dance on stage. This is alright!

That was, until the finale. The underwear throw. Blonde and Brunette allowed their tiny G-strings to slide down their legs and then expertly flicked them off with a stiletto. Seems easy enough. But then, Blonde and Brunette turned to face the back of the stage and bent over. In doing so, they were facing me, and I was confronted with a vagina-related detail I had not previously considered. They were shaved. Totally bald. I. Was. Not.

I could feel the heat rising in my chest and neck. Sometimes I get a heat rash over my neck when I'm nervous. I am guessing at this point, my chest probably looked like the skin of a red leopard. Now, when I say "I wasn't shaved", I'm not talking about that week, or even that month. I had NEVER shaved. Not once. I was presenting to the club, a 1970s situation. A full monster of a bush. Think Australian outback. It was fucking massive. It was like one of those awful dreams where you are naked at school and everyone is laughing. Except it was bloody reality! I was on stage, about to be naked and expose the world's biggest bush. What the fuck was I thinking?!

I took a deep breath, slid my pants down, and got them stuck on my shoe. I had to reach down to yank them off. When I stood up, all I could see were the shoulders. A club full of silhouetted shoulders, bobbing up and down in a unison of giggles. I was mortified. Blonde and Brunette collected their clothes and made for the stage wing. I swiftly followed. Both the girls were very sweet.

"You did great! You're over the first one now. It's easy after that!" Mmm, easy for you to say with your hairless masterpiece of a vagina!

I skulked back to my seat to meet the Australian. "Bravo! You were fantastic!"

He didn't mention my massive bush, and neither did I. Thank God.

From that moment, the rest of the night is somewhat of a blur, but unfortunately, my brain is not on my side, and it remembered all of the worst bits. I drank more champagne. A lot more. I did a few more dances. I sat with the Australian all night. I didn't even get a chance to speak to another man. On around dance number four, I was so blasted that I remember staggering around the stage, falling over and then trying to turn it into some sort of sexy floor move – but instead, I wound up basically rolling around like a pig in mud. I must have looked like an absolute shower of shit. This was confirmed as I left the stage. The club owner, Pete, who I met at my "audition", was standing and waiting in the wings. He started to shout at me, loudly.

"What the fuck are you doing?! You're literally the worst dancer I've ever seen in my life! You're fucked and you can't even walk."

Yep. That's about right. I was greeted by the house mother, who gently took me by the arm and walked me back to the changing rooms.

"Darling! I told you NOT to get drunk! Well, you can't go back out there now. You'll have to sit here until the club closes.

We don't let girls leave on their own early for safety reasons. You'll need to stay here and sober up."

"Okaaay," I slurred quietly.

I was too drunk to do anything other than sit. I remember her bringing me a glass of water and feeding me some ham sandwiches on white bread – it turned out they had plates of sandwiches in the changing rooms every night in case the girls got hungry. Or maybe they were strategically placed to help line their stomachs and prevent them from getting as wasted as I was.

I heard the song "Purple Rain" playing in the club. That was the last song of the night, every night at quarter past three, according to the house mother. I could go home now. Thank God. I took the £300 cash I'd earned and got poured into a taxi, went home to Surbiton and fell into my bed around four in the morning. I woke up with a thumping headache and a feeling of utter embarrassment. I could never ever go back. My one night as a stripper would be my last. Or so I thought.

Almost a year to the day after my big bush bonanza, I was still up shit creek financially. And that night at the strip club had haunted me for a long time. Not just because of the embarrassment, but because I knew that I could do it. I had walked into a situation with no clue what I was doing – I was totally naive and unprepared. But now, I wasn't. Maybe I can go back? No one will recognize me a year down the line. I had since grown my hair long (on my head I mean!) and gotten highlights. And I had shaved! I knew what to wear, and I knew NOT to get shit-faced. Fuck it! I can try again!

And so, I did. I went back to the same strip club, and I became a pretty good stripper! The day I went back, the first girl I met in the club was a five-foot-nothing tiny thing, with bright, red-dyed, curly long hair. She was effervescent, and I instantly fell in love with her. She was a personality like I'd never met before in my life. So bubbly, totally off the wall, and charisma oozed from every pore of her body. After two months at the strip club, she called me one day and told me she had taken an audition at Stringfellows, and I *had* to go with her. "The money is way better, and the club is amazing." So, I did. I spent the next 18 months working there, and they were some of the most fun nights of my life.

The whole experience was empowering. Yes, there were days where I met some total idiots, but I learned so many life skills working in those clubs, and I grew in confidence. I went from a timid mouse to a powerhouse. And this is why I've told this horribly embarrassing story. Well, first and foremost, to give you a giggle, but more importantly, I want to talk about confidence.

On my first day at the strip club, I was desperate for a glass of wine to give me the confidence to get on that stage. What I didn't realize until after I got sober is that confidence is actually somewhat of an illusion. I listen to a lot of self-help-related content, and in early sobriety, I listened to a podcast by Mel Robbins, the famous American self-help guru. She beautifully articulated that all confidence is, is a willingness to try. That's it! It doesn't matter if you feel terrified. You just feel shit-scared and do it anyway.

When I walked into the strip club, got dressed for the night, and put my make-up on, I'd made the decision to get up on that stage. I was confident. I was willing to try. I'd already passed the point of doing something more than merely preparatory. I was there. The alcohol wasn't going to give me confidence. It wasn't going to give me the willingness to try. I had that anyway. What I wanted was simply to shut off the sensation of anxiety. I could get on the stage sober. I just wanted to feel less terrified. We don't use alcohol to become confident – we use it to shut off the feelings of anxiety and panic.

There are so many problems with using booze to dampen feelings of nervousness. Firstly, alcohol causes anxiety. Maybe not at first, but after the cortisol release following glass number one, the net effect of one drink is that once it's worn off, you will always feel worse than before you drank it. Remember what happens after drink one? Dopamine goes up, we feel "relaxed". Cortisol is released, dopamine comes down, cortisol remains. It literally causes stress.

Secondly, our natural stress response is there for a reason! Fight or flight. When you feel nervous before a stressful event, like getting on stage naked, or something slightly more normal, like going for a job interview, your body is preparing you for it by putting you into a state of hypervigilance. This makes us sharper. More aware. By drinking alcohol, we squash this natural response. We become muddled. We're not as sharp. We're dulled. We become less intelligent.

I'm sure you're thinking that it's all well and good to say that you already have confidence simply if you're willing to try, but how does this help during the time when you feel anxious as hell? If you can't use alcohol to take the edge off an intense bout of anxiety, what can you do instead? Mel Robbins had some great advice on this too, in an episode of *The Mel Robbins Podcast* about how to deal with anxiety. When I listened to this particular episode, it was a total light-bulb moment for me. But before I can explain how to deal with anxiety, I first need to talk about a totally different emotion – excitement.

Do you like to feel excited? I'm sure the answer to this is a resounding yes. Me too. I'm a bit of an adrenaline junkie, so I feel most excited when I'm about to do something inherently risky, dangerous or scary. Skydiving is a good example, but for the benefit of everyone reading, I'll use an example that most people should be able to relate to – rollercoasters. Now, granted, some of you may hate rollercoasters! If this is the case, then you can easily substitute this example for anything else that makes you excited. When I'm queuing for a ride that I've not been on before, or one that I have, and I know is terrifying, the first sensation I get in my body is an overall nervous energy, a little like I'm starting to buzz from head to toe. My heart starts to race, I can feel my blood pumping, my chest feels tight, I get hotter, and I feel like my skin is tingling. And it feels good! This nervous energy is the basis of the feeling of excitement.

So how does this relate to dealing with anxiety? Mel Robbins pointed out that the physical sensations caused in our body when we are excited are exactly the same as anxiety. Crazy, right?! How did I not realize this before? They are identical. So why is it that excitement is pleasurable? When I'm very anxious, I feel like I want to rip my own skin off in order to climb out of my own body. Anxiety plagued me for most of my adult life. Anxiety was one of the reasons I drank so much. I just wanted to turn it off and shut it down. All I wanted was to feel less intense, even just for a few hours. Wine did the trick. I needed respite from the wheels turning in my head and the soul-crushing physical symptoms that made me feel like life just wasn't worth living in that state. How can excitement feel so good, and yet the exact same symptoms of anxiety can ruin your life?

Our thoughts. That's it! The thoughts we have in our head dictate whether the feeling we experience in our body is pleasurable or horrific. When we're excited, we enjoy the sensation because we associate the feeling with a positive experience. When we're anxious, we think about something negative. And herein lies the key to managing the symptoms of anxiety. Mel Robbins suggests that we simply change our thoughts, so we turn anxiety into excitement. I found this mind-blowing. What's even more incredible is that it actually works.

I'll give you an example. I hate job interviews – as, I think, most people do. I once did a telephone board interview for a job in Grand Cayman. There were three senior leaders on the end of that call. This was before the days of Skype. It was just me and the phone. I took that interview while chain-smoking Marlboro Lights and drinking Pinot Grigio, while sitting cross-legged on my living room floor. I just wanted to stop the anxiety. Looking back, I can see that the reason I was so nervous, and why so many other people are nervous before interviews, is that I really wanted the job. I was terrified of failing and of not getting to live in the Caribbean. This was my dream job. I wanted it so much that the stakes were incredibly high. If I didn't care about the job, I would undoubtedly have been a lot less anxious. I did actually get the job, but I made some silly errors in that interview because I wasn't sharp. I wasn't on the ball. I would have been if I'd let my anxiety do its job – to put me in fight or flight mode and to make me hyper-aware.

Conversely, I went for a board interview in person more recently where I had to be sober. Rather than be super nervous, I decided to employ the "get excited" tactic. I prepared long and hard. This was key. I knew I would be less anxious if I was well prepared, so this was the first step. Secondly, I thought of all the great things I could think about related to this interview. I fantasized about getting the job, about seeing the extra money on my payslip, about the holiday I would treat myself to when I got the thumbs up. I got excited about showcasing my skills. I thought about telling the interviewers about all my achievements and the projects that I'd completed, which I was super proud of. When I went for the interview, I was prepared – and excited. It completely changed my approach, and it felt a damn sight better than the telephone interview, where I was terrified, unconfident and tipsy. I got the job. I knew I had it in the bag when I walked out of the room. I performed at a totally different level because I exuded confidence. I could feel it.

What would have happened if I hadn't gotten the job? Would all that fantasizing about getting it have been a waste of time? Not at all. I would have been disappointed, yes, but I still would have felt a lot better while going through that process. My job interview wasn't stressful. It was actually quite enjoyable! Put it this way: if you worry about something going wrong and then it does happen, you end up going through the stress of it twice. We can't eliminate all the stressful events in life. It's not possible. There will always be bad days that knock you down. But when we adopt the attitude of "I'll deal with it if and when the bad thing happens", we can at least enjoy life in the spaces in between. And isn't this what we all want? To enjoy life? Courage is simply the willingness to take action. To have a go. Even in the face of fear, you can choose to transform your thoughts into positive ones and turn anxiety into enthusiasm. You can feel joy in adversity. And who doesn't want that?

Harm Reduction – and the Dangers of Switching One Addiction for Another

> "In any moment of decision, the best thing you can do is the right thing, the next best thing is the wrong thing, and the worst thing you can do is nothing."
>
> Theodore Roosevelt

Harm reduction is basically the process of using something that is inherently unhealthy, to quit something that is unhealthier, because it's less damaging. I've already used one example – using sugar to deal with alcohol cravings. We all know that sugar has negative health consequences, but alcohol has far more, and the cost to your physical health is going to be far less by using sugar temporarily. Another example is when people use methadone to come off heroin, in order to lessen the withdrawal symptoms. Harm reduction is useful and helpful for many, but there is a danger of swapping one addiction for another, and this is something I found out the hard way.

The first, secondary addiction I developed – which I didn't even recognize as being an issue until I read a post on a sober group forum from someone else using the same coping mechanism – was shopping! Bear with me, I know this sounds weird. Shopping isn't something that I'd ever really considered to be a "real" addiction. I guess because other than a lower bank balance, I didn't perceive it as causing any harm. It's not *unhealthy* per se, but in early sobriety, shopping quickly became a problem for me because it was totally compulsive and difficult to stop.

In the UK, there is a shopping app called Vinted. It's predominantly used to buy and sell unwanted or second-hand clothes. I bought a brand-new leather jacket with the tags on for £75. The jacket retailed at £400. Bargain! I told myself that since I was saving so much money by not drinking that it was more than justifiable to treat myself. The problem was that I spent about ten times the amount of money that I would have done on alcohol.

Later, I discovered that developing a shopping addiction is really common in early sobriety. Why? Shopping releases the same bloody hormone that alcohol does – dopamine. I was getting a "mini-fix" every time I hit "buy now". I didn't just buy one leather jacket – I bought three. Did I need three leather jackets? Of course not! I also didn't need the countless dresses and pairs of shoes that are now cluttering my wardrobes and rarely see the light of day.

As far as harm reduction goes, shopping isn't the end of the world, and I only spent money that I had. I didn't get into any debt. But there is a far bigger issue here. I was trying to resolve my internal conflict, boredom and unhappiness by using the wrong tools. It would have been easy for my shopping addiction to spiral out of control. Gambling is another common secondary addiction in early sobriety for exactly the same reasons; the brain is seeking out dopamine, and this is an easy way of getting a "quick fix" or a "high".

The second addiction that I developed was far worse: vaping. Within six months of quitting, I was spending more money on vapes than I did on alcohol. My levels of anxiety quickly escalated to ten out of ten within a short space of time. Why did I start vaping? Because many years ago, I used to smoke. On one particular day when I was feeling irritable, I bought a pack of cigarettes. They scratched an itch. I didn't want to get addicted to cigarettes again, so I foolishly decided that vaping would be a good alternative. Vaping, as it turns out, was harder for me to kick than alcohol!

Nicotine works the same way as booze. When your body withdraws, the sensation feels exactly the same as anxiety. When you vape, the feeling of anxiety reduces because you're simply relieving the withdrawal symptoms. It's just another slippery slope, and one that I highly recommend you stay well away from. I found vaping harder to quit than alcohol because there were fewer immediate negative consequences. Vaping didn't give me a hangover. I didn't say or do horrible things when I was vaping. Yes, there were negative consequences for my health, but it was so easy to tell myself that this was just a temporary glitch while I was getting used to sobriety. I would quit soon, and everything would be fine.

When I tried to stop vaping, I realized just how horribly addicted I was. For a start, I was getting through one disposable vape a day – this is the equivalent of smoking 30 cigarettes. I vaped constantly because it was so easy to do so. I didn't need to go outside and light up. I could just keep using it all day long. It became a continuous crutch. When I tried to stop, I felt highly anxious and incredibly irritable. The slightest issue would send me straight back to the local vape shop. I eventually googled and bought Alan Carr's book *How to Quit Vaping*. I had used his book on how to quit smoking many years ago and found it to be instantly successful.

How long does it take nicotine to leave the human body? You're 97 per cent nicotine-free after just six hours. After 48 hours, you're entirely nicotine-free. After the withdrawal period is over you no longer experience physical cravings – much the same as alcohol. Physical cravings are simply the body and mind wanting a substance because it's withdrawing from it – so it feels very much like a need or unstoppable compulsion, not dissimilar to the feelings we get when we're hungry or thirsty. The body believes it needs it to survive. Once you're out of any drugs' withdrawal period, the cravings are all mental, and far less intense. Once you realize that the only reason you feel anxious and *need* to vape is that you're withdrawing, you also realize that vaping is the thing that is keeping you anxious. That's why people sell them – to get you hooked so they can make a profit. If you stop vaping for just a few days, your anxiety will go out the window. It really is that simple.

The reason it's so hard to quit is that you have to experience some short-term discomfort. Alan Carr describes the feeling of nicotine withdrawal as mildly unpleasant, so much so that it doesn't even wake you up at night. It's true, but I felt incredibly anxious and irritable, and it was unpleasant enough that it took me several attempts before I was finally able to kick it. How did I finally quit? I gave myself a bloody good talking-to! Here's what I told myself...

"You do not want to be a vaper. You know this is going to really damage your health in the long run and you need to stop. You quit drinking for fuck's sake! You can do this too. All you need to do is grind out the first week. That's it! This is not a big deal. It's a few days of feeling irritable. It's not painful. It's just annoying! After a week you will have ZERO anxiety. You're anxious BECAUSE you're vaping. You're literally paying money to feel uneasy. Sort your shit out, and just fucking stop!"

Truly, that's all I needed: to sort my shit out and tolerate a few days of feeling a bit uncomfortable. Oh, and I ate my body weight in lollipops. I was constantly sucking one for the first week. Seriously, this is an awesome tool to quit, because when you stop perpetually reaching for a vape pen, with or without the nicotine withdrawal, your brain thinks you're missing something when you don't have one in your hand or your mouth... And for God's sake, if you're in a relationship with a man, don't tell him that you need to keep your mouth and your hands busy – you know damn well what he'll suggest. I don't even know why it's called a blow job – I have never been paid for this work. Come to think of it, unless you're a prostitute who at least has the good sense to get rewarded monetarily for her efforts, I think we should all start referring to this act as a "volunteer blow". Stick to lollipops – far less work and they taste way better. I digress.

A few days of feeling mildly uncomfortable and irritable is not a big sacrifice. I promise you, you'll feel a million times better once the first week is over. Vaping causes the very problem it relieves, just like alcohol. Stop for even a week and you can see and feel the benefits. It's not really a long time at all. Yes, you'll feel tetchy and irritable – but if you can keep telling yourself that this will subside in just one week, it helps to know there is a short end date.

If you're currently trying to quit alcohol or considering doing so, try to be aware of any other unhealthy behaviours you might begin to engage in. They're all driven by the same underlying impulse – avoidance and escapism. We try to hide from difficult emotions because we don't want to face them. The only way to overcome this is to go through it. Feeling your emotions is the key to dealing with them. Only by truly listening to ourselves can we know what we need to focus on.

Harm reduction can be helpful, but not if it creates a bigger problem. Reaching for a bag of Haribo is one thing, but be careful not to turn to other drugs. They all create the same problem. Regardless of the drug, the withdrawal symptoms are the opposite of the drug's effects. The result is more anxiety and a whole host of other health issues. There is no good that can come from it. With any drug, it will always take more than it gives. You will always wind up feeling worse afterwards.

Getting High

I know a man who went through rehab and is now a couple of years sober. He didn't have a drug of choice. He loved them all. He describes himself as a "wreck head" – a term he attributed to himself because if any drug was put in front of him, he would take it and abuse it, regardless of what it was. The first time I heard this term it resonated a little too deeply, for I am most certainly a "wreck head".

I'm writing this chapter having already finished penning this book, because I was in two minds about whether to touch on the subject of drug abuse. Addiction is a term used for both alcohol and drugs, but from my own experience, these substances are entirely different beasts. What's more, I feel that drug abuse needs an entire book to itself, just to cover its sheer complexity. Yet because it was a significant aspect of my recovery journey, I can well imagine it will be the same for many other people. Especially if you're a fellow "wreck head".

Alcohol was never my drug of choice. I didn't like that it turned me into a raging moron, I couldn't bear feeling hungover and I hated the fact it would make me say and do things that were so incongruent with my values. Drugs, on the other hand, often made me a better person (I'll explain shortly) – particularly opiates. Now when I refer to my personal experience with drug abuse, I'm not talking about scoring on street corners and sitting in a shitty crack den. For the last three decades I've had multiple dealers and they all had one thing in common – they were called Doctor.

Now, I'm not saying that all doctors are potential dealers – far from it. It's difficult to get *most* doctors to prescribe anything addictive, but there are always going to be those few who are easy to manipulate, and I sniffed them out like a bloodhound on a scent trail. I vividly remember the first time I realized that you could use a doctor to "score". I was 15 years old and a school friend told me that she had been prescribed Valium (diazepam), because she was scared of flying. My immediate first thought – I need to get to a doctor and say the same thing. Ironically, at the time, I wasn't scared of flying – but now I'm terrified! I have quite happily thrown myself out of a plane at 13,000 feet, but I don't like sitting on a commercial flight at all – a fear that has been ever-present since I took a flight on 12 September after the fateful events of 9/11.

I managed to get my hands on some diazepam with minimal effort. Sure enough, a doctor was quite happy to prescribe it, given my "fear". It's now almost impossible to get this drug from an NHS doctor because it's highly addictive and massively abused, so they're very reluctant to prescribe it. I absolutely understand why – it's lovely. A pill that makes you feel instantly relaxed and fuzzy without all the negative side effects of alcohol. The only downside was that it would also make me feel very sleepy. (There is little point in taking a drug if you're missing out on the effects because you're getting some shut-eye.) It also doesn't last very long, so you need to keep taking it to maintain the fuzzy sensation – and because doctors don't like giving out loads of the stuff, it's short-lived.

Diazepam was my introduction to the world of prescription meds but, needless to say, it didn't stop there. I've known and loved most of them. Diazepam, lorazepam, temazepam, codeine, pregabalin, zopiclone, tramadol, morphine and oxycodone – these are just my favourites. Since the birth of my first son, it's been easy to get my hands on most of these drugs because I have ulcerative colitis. Ironically, I have actually needed these drugs rather than just wanted them, because I get joint pain so severe that the only way I can describe it is to say it feels like I've been shot in the kneecaps – well, I presume that's what getting shot feels like. And because I needed them, I know all too well just how addictive they are, and how desperately difficult they are to stop.

You see, alcohol is actually quite easy on the body to stop. Mentally, it's a bitch, and the journey is long, but physically, unless you're hellishly addicted and drinking in the morning, the symptoms of withdrawal are more than tolerable. Plus, there is a far greater driving force to quit than with drugs – because alcohol has such a vast number of negative side effects.

The problem with opiates (painkillers derived from opium) and barbiturates (sedatives derived from barbituric acid) is that there is very little to no downside when you're actually taking them. They only become an issue when you stop. When you can't get any more and have to withdraw. Coming off opiates is like taking a slow walk through hell.

During one particularly nasty colitis flare-up, my sister was staying with me one weekend and I had to get her to call 111 to get an emergency prescription, as the doctor's office was closed. My joints were so painful that I couldn't walk, talk or even move from the sofa. I just sat and wailed in total agony. I would have taken absolutely anything I was given by a doctor, and the morphine I was prescribed quickly did the trick. Not only did morphine rapidly decrease my pain levels, it also gave me a tremendous sense of well-being. Like looking at the world through rose-tinted glasses and spending my days wrapped in invisible cotton wool. I felt more loving and caring. I also remember buying a lot of gifts for people. It quite literally made me a nicer person. I LOVED it.

The other great thing about morphine is that it lasts much longer than barbiturates, for example diazepam. The problem only comes when you try to stop. Firstly, coming off morphine can cause a lot of physical pain, so as soon as I tried to stop taking it, my joints would become incredibly painful. At the time, I had no idea that morphine withdrawal actually causes joint pain, so I naturally thought that the pain I was feeling continued to be colitis-related – so I just kept taking it. I had slow-release morphine tablets and liquid morphine on a repeat prescription. There wasn't a chance in hell I was coming off that stuff while I had free access to it.

It was only when I stopped drinking and started to read about all types of addiction that I realized the morphine I was taking was causing the problem it claimed to relieve. It only came to a head when I went on holiday and mistakenly didn't take enough with me to last until I got home, so I had to ration the morphine for the duration of the trip, so that I didn't start to withdraw.

Decreasing my dose didn't cause me to start clucking – but it did make me feel depressed as hell. I started to realize the massive impact this drug was having on my body and my mind. Bolstered by my recent sobriety from alcohol and the newfound knowledge that the morphine was causing more harm than good, when I got home, I decided to quit cold turkey – a foolish decision that I came to regret very quickly. The recommendation is to taper off it – and with good reason. I had read that tapering is less painful, but the pain lasts much longer. I just wanted it done and dusted. I knew it was going to be difficult, so I contacted the doctor's office and asked them to take the morphine off my repeat list. I didn't want to be tempted to get more of it and I was not going to fail. I took my last dose first thing in the morning. By five in the afternoon, I started to rattle more than a poisonous snake.

The first thing I noticed was that the lovely sense of well-being turned into a prolonged and ultra-intense panic attack. I felt so incredibly anxious that I could barely tolerate it. But the anxiety was a non-event compared to the physical pain I had to endure for the next 48 hours. I couldn't sit still. I'd heard of the expression "kicking the habit" when referring to heroin withdrawal, but I didn't know why that phrase existed. As it turns out, when you come off morphine, you can't keep your legs still, so you end up violently and repeatedly kicking out until the withdrawal period ends – hence "kicking the habit". It's really hard to explain exactly how this feels, but it's kind of like having a constant twitch that's excruciatingly painful. Almost like an alien had hijacked my body and was trying to escape by breaking through my skin. I tried to go to sleep but it was physically impossible to lie in bed without thrashing around. I got up and paced around the house for the entire night. I was exhausted and all I wanted to do was sleep, but I couldn't stay still, even for a few seconds. Then came the stomach ache. Crippling cramping that left me doubled over. My joints ached like my bones had been injected with poison. It felt like every organ in my body was pulsating and slowly dying. I felt like I would die. Had I been able to access morphine at that point, I would certainly have necked it.

Coming off that drug was one of the worst experiences of my life and I often wonder how anyone comes back from a heroin addiction. I was taking prescription-strength morphine – which is a fraction of the strength of heroin – and I felt like dying. Coming off heroin must feel like getting tortured by the devil himself. Anyone who recovers should be given a medal.

While I've never taken heroin, I can imagine how it feels, having once been prescribed "hillbilly heroin" – oxycodone – also derived from the opium poppy. The only difference is that one is made by doctors and scientists, while the other is made on the street. It was 2012 and I was living in Grand Cayman at the time. All drugs on the island were imported from the US, and unbeknown to me at that time, oxycodone was causing a nationwide opioid crisis, which still exists today. Thankfully the drug is only prescribed in the UK for palliative care. If it was readily available, I wouldn't be here to write this book, and to this day, I don't think I would be able to resist taking it if it was put in front of me. This drug is pure evil.

I woke up one day with a raging toothache and promptly took myself off to the dentist. I was prescribed some codeine and antibiotics before I was sent on my way. I had an impacted, infected wisdom tooth. It would settle in a few days, I was told. Twenty-four hours later, I felt like I'd been hit around the face with a baseball bat. I've never experienced toothache like that before. I went back to the dentist in floods of tears. I was prescribed a drug with the brand name Endocet and told "this is a really good painkiller and it will make you feel much better". I'd never heard of it. I certainly didn't think to look it up on Google and I took two pills without a second thought. Those two pills could have eventually, and easily, cost me my life. I was instantaneously hooked to a drug I didn't even know existed.

About ten minutes before the drug took effect, I vividly recall being sat on my sofa and holding my face in pain. As the drug began to course through my veins, I took hold of my head in both hands and I shouted "Fuuuuuuuccccccckkkkkkk" out loud. I'd never felt anything like it. It blew my head off. It was the most incredible, instant, completely overwhelming high I'd ever experienced. Oxycodone made me feel invincible. Nothing could hurt me – the world was beautiful. I felt intense feelings of love for everyone around me and it lasted for a good eight hours solid. This was my drug of choice. This is my drug of choice.

I went back to the dentist, specifically to get more oxy. Then I went to my doctor and made multiple excuses as to why I needed further repeat prescriptions. I get horrendous migraines. I suffer from back pain. I have another toothache. I managed to get another five or six prescriptions and I spent my days in oxy-heaven. I've never felt so at peace with the world and in love with my life. This was the answer to every problem I'd ever had.

I stopped drinking alcohol. Oxycodone made alcohol seem like the shittest drug ever. Ironic that it took one of the worst and strongest drugs there is to give me a period of sobriety from alcohol. At the time, I wholeheartedly believed it was a far healthier alternative. It removed the chaos and destruction caused by alcohol and left me feeling better than I'd ever felt.

Luckily, the last doctor I saw to try to get an oxy prescription had some knowledge of the opiate crisis. He saw straight through me and said, "You have to stop taking this. It's insanely addictive and it will eventually kill you. It's an awful drug. No one should take it." He made sure I couldn't ask for it again by writing up my notes accordingly. I was angry at the time. Actually, not angry – I was livid. This total twat was the only thing standing between me and my new beautiful world. If I saw him now, I'd give him a cuddle and profusely thank him for saving my life. He stopped me early enough that I wasn't physically dependent and I didn't have any withdrawal symptoms.

If I saw the dentist who prescribed me oxycodone for a toothache, I'd struggle not to punch him in the face. The irresponsibility of prescribing this drug for any condition is astounding, but for a toothache, it should be made a criminal offence. I've often wondered how many addicts this utter twonk of a dentist has created. How many lives have been lost over a toothache? I was addicted to alcohol, but I can now be around it easily as I no longer have any desire to drink. I see no value in it. I can't say the same for oxycodone. With full understanding of the utter devastation this drug causes and the knowledge that a prescription for oxy is tantamount to a death sentence, I would still struggle to refuse it if put in front of me. That's how addictive it is. I thank my lucky stars that I don't live in America. If I lived there, I would die there. Very quickly.

I made my mind up that I would never take morphine again, regardless of the pain I was in. I couldn't go through that horrendous experience again. Several months later, during my next painful colitis flare-up, I googled for any and every natural remedy I could get my hands on. Folic acid, vitamin D, omega oil, aloe vera gel, high-potency turmeric. The list goes on. I'm sure some of this helped a little, but it was an article on medical cannabis that sparked my interest. Apparently, there are only four conditions eligible for medical cannabis on a private prescription – and colitis is one of them. Excellent!

I smoked a lot of weed in my late teens and recall thoroughly enjoying myself, laughing frequently and eating vast amounts of cookies. I could also pick it up and put it down no problem. I never felt or became addicted and stopped with no issues at the grand old age of 21. This could be my new pain relief and it was entirely natural and available on prescription! What a perfect solution!

I contacted a private medical company that dealt (no pun intended) exclusively in medical cannabis prescriptions. I completed the answers to a series of questions and within a couple of days I received an email to confirm I was indeed eligible, and a Zoom meeting was arranged for me to speak with a private doctor. Half an hour later I had some cannabis oil and cannabis flowers being sent to my house by courier. When the prescription arrived, I was expecting medical cannabis to look completely different to the street version. I don't know why. I presumed that if it's prescribed, it would look like, well, a prescription. Nope. I had been sent two pots of some high-potency, very strong-smelling skunk. Just as I remembered it from over two decades ago. Aah. The smell of my youth.

The doctor advised that I was to put a tiny amount of oil under my tongue and it would take a couple of hours to work. The cannabis flowers were for vaping. I'd never even heard of a dry herb vape. It is still illegal to smoke cannabis in the UK, even when on prescription. Vaping, however, causes the flowers to be heated and then only the vapour is ingested. Far healthier than smoking the stuff as there is no tobacco used. Fabulous. This saved having to remember how to roll joints. I'm pretty sure I've lost that skill after 20 years.

I tried the oil first. It tasted utterly disgusting. After a couple of hours, I couldn't feel any effects, so I used the vape for the first time. The effects of this were instant. And then the oil began to kick in – I hadn't appreciated there would be a delayed reaction. Now, as luck would have it, I was child-free for my baptism into the world of prescription cannabis. Lucky, because I wasn't capable of stringing a sentence together, let alone looking after my children. I was an instant space cadet. It felt like I wasn't in my own body. I can vividly recall washing my hair and getting confused as it felt like someone else was washing it for me. My hands seemed disconnected somehow. Then came the paranoia.

I went to my kitchen to make some hot lemon and cut a slice on the chopping board. Suddenly my brain went into paranoid overdrive. What if I accidentally cut off my fingers because I'm too stoned to be careful? What if I start bleeding out and I don't even notice? Oh shit! I could die today! All because I cut a lemon! It turns out that getting high is not quite how I remember it. Funny how I only seem to recall the good bits. I'd envisaged sitting around giggling and eating a few too many cookies, all while simultaneously getting my colitis into remission and living a glorious pain-free existence. Reality was somewhat far removed from the fantasy.

I had to be really careful when I took this drug, because I simply couldn't function like a responsible adult, let alone a parent, when I'd taken the oil. I took a dose right after the school run so that I would be functioning by school pickup time. The problem was, I still had to work from home. I lost count of the amount of Microsoft Teams meetings I attended where halfway through a sentence I would declare, "Oh, I'm so sorry. I've completely forgotten what I was talking about."

Words literally fell out of my head. Words weren't the only thing to go walkabout. My common sense fucked off at the exact same time.

I sent Arthur to the end of the road to post a couple of birthday cards and forgot to put the stamps on them – so my friends had to pay the post office charges in order to collect them. I screwed up my online food shop because I was so off the planet and distracted that I forgot half the things I needed. I became absolutely incapable of multitasking. Being stoned must be what it feels like to be a man: only able to manage one task at a time and even then, totally fucking it up. I jest of course, but it's incredible to me that such a tiny amount of THC could render me absolutely useless.

My memories of smoking weed as a teenager are delightful. The problem is that the passage of time causes memories to be incredibly rose-tinted and a far cry from reality. Just as they are with alcohol. Time is a fantastic healer, because all of the bad stuff is minimized – which is great until you're trying to remember exactly where you don't want to be. Part of the reason that my recollections of getting high are so lovely is that during the time I was using weed, I had zero responsibility. I was a student. Aside from studying, I had very little else that I needed my brain to be straight for. Getting fucked-up midweek was a non-event. It turns out that getting high when you've got two kids to look after, a full-time job and a house to run isn't much fun. It's basically parenting while paranoid with an added dose of stress – because no one can multitask when their brain is on the blink and everything goes to shit!

To be fair, the cannabis did work for my joint aches because you can't feel pain in your limbs if it doesn't feel like your legs are even attached to your body. Nonetheless, my dabble with prescription weed didn't last very long. Paranoia and ineptitude aside, the worst thing about taking it was that I wasn't clear-headed. I didn't feel like myself. And I'd grown to love feeling sober. What I'd failed to realize is that giving up alcohol had got me so accustomed to reality that I'd grown to dislike the escape. I like being in control of my mind. I need to be on the ball, and I'm so happy that I am. My hazy rose-tinted memories of smoking weed while listening to acoustic guitar and giggling with my friends are a warped recollection of my past – and that's exactly where they need to stay. I was shocked at just how much I'd come to rely on and love being completely sober.

I genuinely believed that prescription weed would be awesome. Of course I did. My addict brain loves any suggestion of taking a chemical substance. A way to have a little escape from reality and alleviate my colitis symptoms, without needing to resort to morphine. In actuality, it was a total let-down. My memories didn't match reality at all. When life is good, you don't need to escape it and anything that allows you to escape generally has a plethora of downsides.

The only drug I now take is paracetamol, and even then, sporadically. The best solution for my joint pain is prevention rather than cure. I look after my body. I exercise and eat cleanly. When I have a flare-up and my joints are painful, I can actually tolerate it much better than I ever realized before. I was always so quick to reach for a pill that I didn't give my body any time to recover on its own. Of course, there will be times when medication is essential, and I'm certainly not advocating avoiding a doctor or prescription meds, but I do think it's worth asking yourself whether you are taking a prescription because you need it or because you want it. Reality takes some getting used to, but there is no drug like navigating your life with ease and feeling confident and competent enough to deal with challenges on your own.

One of the reasons I decided to write this chapter is to show just how ridiculous and pointless alcohol is as a drug. There are so many downsides. Addiction to opiates makes sense to me – because they do feel great, they last a long time and you don't suffer until you stop using them. That's why they're so tough to quit. But alcohol? Alcohol ruins your life, even when you're taking it! How ludicrous is a drug that only makes you feel good for a tiny period of time before it makes you feel terrible and turns you into a dickhead? It's rubbish!

So why is alcohol the drug of choice for so many people? Two reasons. It's legal and it's accessible. In the UK, it's very difficult to get prescribed controlled drugs, even with a medical condition. Alcohol can be bought anywhere, at any time. Because it's legal and socially endorsed, there is an air of acceptability around consuming it. You've only got a problem if you come out and say you've got a problem.

Alcohol became a problem for me because it was the only drug that I had free and constant access to. It was my fallback remedy, and the equivalent of having my own private doctor on speed dial. Booze has so many disadvantages and it was never my drug of choice, but at least I never had to worry about running out. I would always choose prescription medication over a drink given the choice, because I felt that there were far fewer downsides.

There is undeniably an added complexity to quitting any substance if you're abusing more than one at the same time, and this needs to be treated with the utmost caution. When I quit drinking, I was also using liquid morphine, which as I mentioned earlier, was extremely difficult to stop and something I tackled after I became sober from alcohol. I knew the booze needed to go first, because it was causing me far more issues, both mentally and physically. So how do you tackle multiple addictions? Firstly, it depends on how many substances you're taking and the nature of the drugs themselves. An addiction to crystal meth is an entirely different beast to a benzodiazepine habit. Each drug has different withdrawal symptoms and different risks, so with any complex addiction, the first step should always be to visit your doctor. At least then you can be advised on how dangerous it is to stop, what the withdrawal from each substance will look like, and whether or not it's sensible to tackle one at a time, or all together in a detox clinic. It's super common for people to abuse more than one substance at a time. Why? Because they all do the same thing – kill pain temporarily – and often one drug can relieve the withdrawal symptoms of another. Morphine is a great way to cure a hangover headache (and was how I tackled the school run). The epitome of using a sledgehammer to crack a nut. Heroin is great if you're coming down off cocaine. As soon as you feel pain from one drug's withdrawal, you need another substance to take the edge off. This is one reason alcohol is a gateway to other drugs and why addiction as a whole is one massive slippery slope.

As I've already mentioned, though, the great thing about quitting alcohol is that if you're not physically dependent, it's not *that* difficult to stop. Withdrawal is mildly uncomfortable but you quickly recover and feel so much better within a relatively short space of time. In fact, within just two weeks you look and feel like an entirely different person. Mentally, yes, it's a hurdle, but if you know and understand the process of quitting, it really is far easier to navigate. Remember, when you cease to see value in a drug, you simply won't crave it.

If alcohol is your only drug of choice, ask yourself what you get from using it, and what it takes from you. The latter list will be far more extensive. Compared to the countless other drugs out there, it's got the least benefits and some of the biggest risks. Giving up alcohol is not giving up anything. It's just removing something that causes countless problems and makes you feel completely terrible. It's shit at its job as a drug! The equivalent of a rock star playing the triangle or a dentist pulling out a tonsil instead of a tooth. The only real benefit of alcohol is how great you feel once you give it up for good.

Alcohol and Anxiety

> "Anxiety does not empty tomorrow of its sorrows,
> but only empties today of its strength."
>
> Alexander Maclaren

I always believed myself to be an anxious person. I thought that anxiety was somehow part of my genetic make-up. There wasn't anything I could do about it. I worried a lot. That was just who I was. After about one week alcohol-free, I discovered that I wasn't so anxious after all. The intense and sometimes crippling anxiety I experienced on a daily basis was most likely just a withdrawal symptom. This was a huge revelation to me and also quite a depressing discovery. I had spent the best part of 25 years in a needless state of perpetual stress. When I look back, I can remember being relatively anxiety-free until I was about 15 years old. Incidentally, this was around the age when I started frequently drinking socially. What could my life have looked like had I never picked up a drink? How many unnecessary stressful days could have been avoided? After a while I had to force myself to stop asking myself these sorts of questions – they were just too depressing.

I spent the first couple of months of sobriety in a state of peace. Bored as shit, granted, but peaceful nonetheless. Then something rather annoying happened – my anxiety levels began to increase again. After the withdrawal period ends, the body breathes a sigh of relief – a few weeks later once the equilibrium has been established, your true levels of anxiety come to light. I tried exercising, meditation, journalling, yoga, medication and listening to podcasts. Nothing worked. I couldn't for the life of me work out why I felt so mentally wired all the time. Why did I constantly feel like I was on the precipice of a heart attack? It couldn't be the alcohol. That was long out of my system.

I came across a book called *Mind Control*, written by a man named José Silva. Silva was an electronics repairman who developed an interest in psychology to see if he could raise his children's IQ. He became convinced that he had taught his daughter to become clairvoyant and subsequently decided to learn more about the development of psychic abilities.

Hear me out. I'm not about to tell you that I cured my anxiety by becoming a psychic!

Silva developed a method of mind control known widely as the Silva Method. The method is designed so that a person can learn to control their mind and reach an enhanced state of awareness in order to mentally project with a specific intent and connect with higher intelligence. A little like the law of attraction, the aim is to focus on what you want in order to get what you want, with the premise that thoughts become actions and actions change your life (with a touch of help from the universe). I'm still not sure if I believe in the method or the powers of mind control to influence the universe, but there was one section of the book that was so illuminating to me that it started a lengthy journey of my own discovery into what anxiety actually is and how it can be reduced.

Silva uses an example to show the incredible power of the human mind. I love the example because it's solid proof that thoughts can cause physiological changes in the body. Our thoughts can literally do us harm – or good for that matter. The example used involves imagining eating a lemon, and you can easily try the exercise yourself.

Close your eyes and imagine walking into your kitchen and taking a lemon from the sideboard, or wherever you would normally keep lemons. Imagine taking the lemon in your hand and feeling the waxy skin. Now smell it. Concentrate on how the lemon feels when you put it to your lips. Spend a couple of minutes thinking about this. Now take a knife from your kitchen and cut the lemon on a chopping board. Imagine picking up the lemon and feel how it becomes wet in your hands as the juice starts to flow out. Lift the lemon up to your face and imagine squeezing the juice into your mouth. Think about how bitter it is. How sour. Swill the juice around in your mouth. If you really concentrate you will notice something remarkable starts to happen – you will begin to salivate. Incredible, right? There is no real lemon, yet your brain can tap into the memory and recreate the same physiological response as if the lemon were actually real. Your body can produce excess saliva just by thinking about the memory of previously eating a lemon.

The same thing happens to me when I think about nails being scratched down a blackboard. I get chills down my spine. Or if

I think about chewing on tin foil – ugh! That's giving me shivers as I write this. Now consider that the human mind has between 12,000 and 60,000 thoughts a day. How many physiological reactions can your body have to that many thoughts? A lot!

The example of the lemon clearly proves that our thoughts cause our body to physically react – so how does this relate to anxiety? Anxiety is caused by our own thoughts. I didn't like learning this. I wanted to reject the notion. To accept it would mean that I basically spend most of my life mentally self-harming. I don't want to have thoughts that cause me to feel anxious. I hate feeling anxious. Okay, maybe my thoughts did cause me to feel panic, but my thoughts would flood in thick and fast. I didn't choose them; they happened to me. Didn't they?

During my period of research into anxiety, I decided to have some intensive one-on-one therapy. The therapy I tried was similar to CBT (cognitive behavioural therapy). If my brain really was to blame for the anxiety I had experienced for so long, then speaking to someone about what my thoughts actually were seemed as good a place to start as any. Without delving into several weeks of self-analysis, what I did learn is that thoughts are chosen by us, and although they can be difficult to actually master, they are somewhat controllable.

I historically adopted certain habitual thinking patterns that were largely unhelpful and common among those of us who suffer from anxiety. The most significant pattern is asking myself the question "What if?" several thousand times a day. For every worry I have, I think of every possible catastrophic outcome. For years I have unconsciously held the belief that worrying will, in some way, protect me from the future. If I worry about every eventuality of a problem and plan as much as possible for the worst-case scenario, then maybe if the event happens, I'll be better prepared for it. Of course, this is nonsense. But it's been a tough habit to break.

Worrying about an event in the future means I effectively go through double the amount of stress. If the negative event happens, worrying about it beforehand doesn't prepare me in any way. There are things I can do to prepare, but fretting about it is not one of them. Agonizing over the future just means I feel like I've been through the drama twice over. Sometimes I worry, and the event never even happens. But it may as well have because I've effectively experienced it anyway, by feeling the stress in advance. Ruminating on potential future negative outcomes doesn't achieve anything other than making us feel anxious in the here and now.

I've learned that I only have control over two things in this life: what I think and what I do. That's literally it. When I worry, I now ask myself if there is anything I can do to prepare myself. Is there any action I can take here and now? If the answer is yes, I simply get on with it. If the answer is no, I tell myself, "There is nothing you can do. You'll deal with the outcome when you get there, like you always do and have done – with every other problem you've ever had before." More often than not, my worries never even come to fruition. When they do, I deal with them. And you do too. Every single problem you've ever had in this life you've dealt with, because you're still here, still standing. And for every problem that arises in the future, you will deal with them when you get there.

Anxiety was one of the many reasons I drank alcohol. My brain was on a repeated thought loop, agonizing over every potential problem I might come across in the future. Alcohol shut that down. It was a quick way to turn my mind off, to slow the dreaded mental hamster wheel constantly turning around in my head. I found sobriety really tough in the first few months when I felt anxious. I didn't like sitting with my feelings and thoughts. I just wanted my brain to shut the fuck up!

Let me be clear, I have not gained complete mastery over my thought process, and my brain continues to conjure up worst-case scenarios at times. But what I've found is that when these thoughts do arise, I can see them for what they are and consciously interrupt them. I can replace negative thoughts with positive ones. The shift in perception doesn't even need to be significant. It's just about using words that are kinder, like you would talk to a friend. The way I used to speak to myself was downright unfriendly! I would tell myself that my life was falling apart, I was terrible at everything, and I would never be able to cope. It simply wasn't helpful.

The shifts in my thinking are sometimes really subtle. I can't tell myself that everything is fantastic when I'm feeling rubbish. I simply won't believe it. But I can lessen the blow. Instead of telling myself, "Today was so shit. Why does everything always go wrong? Things will never get better," I shift my perspective and apply a positive spin. "Today wasn't great. It's not ideal when things go wrong, but sometimes I have days where everything feels easier. That's life. Things always get better. Today was bad, but it's just one day. Good ones will follow."

I now consciously apply these shifts in thinking, every hour of every day. Sometimes my mind runs away and starts to catastrophize, but I can see when it's happening, and I choose to replace my negative thoughts with positive ones. When I was drinking, my problems would always be waiting for me in the morning. I may have shut my brain off for a while, but it was temporary. The following day I'd still have the same issues – but I'd also be nursing a hangover and withdrawal symptoms, which only make anxiety worse.

Anxiety is caused by an underestimation of our ability to cope in the future. When we look at our problems and face them, we feel resourceful and empowered. Drinking is a great way to mentally bury your worries for a while – but it doesn't solve anything. Taking action, being prepared where we can, and replacing our negative thoughts with more positive ones are soothing and useful.

When you think about squeezing a lemon into your mouth, you salivate. When you worry about the future, you induce feelings of panic. When you actively resolve your problems, your body also responds accordingly. We have much more control over our thoughts than we think, and therefore the ability to rapidly and significantly reduce our own anxiety.

One of the reasons I've spent a phenomenal amount of time asking myself "what if?" and worrying about the future is that I've been very intolerant of uncertainty. I like and want to feel safe. The reality is that life is uncertain. There are zero guarantees for the future, except to say that we will all end up six feet under. What happens before that is anyone's guess. Uncertainty can feel terrifying, but it can also feel exciting. How much fun would life be if we all knew exactly what path it would take? It would be boring as hell! Part of the beauty of life is that anything can happen. We weather the bad stuff so we can enjoy the great times. You can choose to look at uncertainty as something to be feared or something to be embraced.

For every bad experience I've had in this life, a good one has followed. Think of life as a wheel. When you get to the top, you're in a place where you're loving life and riding high. But that wheel is forever turning. When we're on top, the natural trajectory is that we must come down, as certain as gravity. Bad times will follow. When we're at rock bottom, sitting uncomfortably at the base of the wheel, it can only go up. The good times are coming. And so, the cycle begins again.

What I've noticed in sobriety is that my own wheel has changed in pace and size. When I was drinking, I would feel huge highs and soul-crushing lows. The wheel was so big that when I fell from the top, it felt like I'd thrown myself off a building and landed with a thud. I also spent a lot more time at the bottom of the wheel. I felt miserable for most of the time. The wheel turned slowly when I was at the bottom. In sobriety, my wheel is much smaller. The lows are never as low, and the wheel turns much quicker. When I'm at the bottom, I can be at the top again in a few short hours. I can have a bad morning, but recover much quicker and be feeling great again by the afternoon. When I fall from the top of the wheel, I don't have far to fall. I land with a little bump, and I've got this awesome super-thick crash mat so I don't really hurt myself – sobriety.

Alcohol kept me stuck at the bottom of the wheel, and a bad day could turn into a bad month. The wheel was vicious and often frightening, like a fairground ride that needed some serious repairs – it was downright dangerous. My sober wheel is like a kids' ride. Even if it breaks down for a while, I can climb down safely enough, and there is always another solution because I'm not living in alcohol-induced chaos.

Alcohol does a great job of switching your mind off from your worries, but they will always be waiting for you in the morning. In sobriety, you can learn to listen to yourself and deal with the problems you're facing head-on, and inevitably, the anxiety reduces. Try replacing your worries with kinder language. The words we use are powerful, and they become our lived experience of reality. Tell yourself that your current situation is a "fucking nightmare", and it will feel like one. Your body physically responds to the thoughts in your head. Tell yourself that you have a "bit of a hurdle", and your body will react to this in a far less aggressive way. We have way more control over our emotional state than we often believe. We can induce calm in the same way we can induce internal panic.

What problems do you currently have going on in your life? Do they feel like a fucking nightmare or a bit of a hurdle? However you feel about your current situation, this is just your interpretation and experience of it, and the beauty of this is that it can be changed. I'll give you an example of a very minor problem I have right now. As I'm typing, my tumble dryer is grinding away and making an awfully loud noise. I'm surprised my neighbours haven't complained. The noise is pissing me off, firstly because it's annoying, and secondly because the machine is only two years old, and I've just had to buy a replacement that will arrive tomorrow. I was annoyed to have to make this purchase. How would you react in this circumstance? You might not be bothered at all. You might be financially well off, and a broken tumble dryer may be just a minor inconvenience. It might absolutely incense you because now you need to pay out for something unexpectedly, and a tumble dryer should last a lot more than two years. You may have five children and exorbitant amounts of laundry on a daily basis – this might feel very disruptive and stressful for you. I have chosen to think about someone who doesn't have a tumble dryer because they can't afford one. How would they feel about my situation? They may think I should be grateful for having a tumble dryer in the first place. What about someone who doesn't have a home? How would they view my problem? They probably wouldn't view it as a problem at all. It's not essential; I've got a roof over my head. I'm extremely lucky. My tumble dryer issue is a non-event – because I've chosen to view it that way.

Our experience of life is observed and felt through the lens we choose for ourselves. We have the power to change that lens at any time. Right now, I have a choice: I can choose to be annoyed, or I can choose to be incredibly grateful that I have a beautiful home and the means to replace my tumble dryer. If we approach our lives with eternal gratitude for the blessings we do have, everything looks better through that lens, especially through a sober one. I choose to be optimistic because quite simply, it feels better.

Sobriety and Motherhood

> "There is no way to be a perfect mother,
> but a million ways to be a good one."

Jill Churchill

When I thought about becoming a mother, I had a vision of what that would look like. I imagined bringing a child into the world would be a magical and wonderful experience. Instead, my journey into motherhood was a baptism of fire I could only have dreamt of in my nightmares. I had a picture-perfect pregnancy (aside from severe morning sickness in the early months) and fully expected labour to be painful – but I didn't expect it to go so horribly wrong.

I was living in Grand Cayman at the time. The hospital procedure was to induce, as my son was a week late. I was in excruciating pain by five centimetres dilated – so I opted for an epidural. As I came closer to the ten-centimetre mark, the epidural failed. I went from no pain to ten out of ten pain, very quickly. I couldn't speak at all. I couldn't articulate that I didn't know when to push, because the pain was constant. All I could do was to cry and scream in agony. My son started to crown, but he became stuck. After a failed vacuum, I was rushed down for an emergency caesarean. I was put under general anaesthetic in the midst of utter commotion. Doctors everywhere – all panicking. When I woke, I was scared to ask if my son was alive. I was so sure he wouldn't be. I was quickly told by the doctor that my son, Arthur, was in the ICU and was stable – but he was born blue and it took four minutes to resuscitate him. I'm grateful I was unconscious at the time. Unbeknown to me, I was close to dying myself. I'd lost a lot of blood and had some blood transfusions. It was touch and go for a while apparently. I was then told that Arthur was so stuck during delivery that to get him out, they had to make a vertical incision down my belly so they could pull him out by his feet.

Those first few days in hospital were equally delightful and harrowing. Delightful because Arthur was the most precious, beautiful baby. Harrowing because I was traumatized by the birth. I suffered with post-partum psychosis. I could hear the nurses talking in the next room. They were discussing that my son had died and I'd had a hysterectomy – but they were scared to tell me in case I killed myself. I confronted the nurse in outrage when she came into my room. The conversation had never happened. I was in such a traumatized state that I was suffering audio hallucinations. I could hear music that wasn't actually playing. It was so strange to know that it was in my mind, but I was able to hear it nonetheless.

When we went home, I thought my ordeal was over. Little did I know, it had just begun. After a couple of days at home, I started to experience contractions again. They became so severe, so quickly, that I collapsed and was rushed back to hospital. After days of exams, blood tests and prodding around, the surgeon advised I would need another operation – a laparotomy. I'd developed a huge internal infection that needed to be removed and drained. After surgery, I spent ten days in hospital. I wasn't allowed to have Arthur stay with me – he could only visit for a few hours during the day. I also wasn't allowed to breastfeed during that time either because of the medication I was taking – this was heart-breaking and utterly distressing for me at that time.

The surgical wound on my stomach was vertical and spanned ten inches. The incision was stapled back together and left open, to reduce the risk of another infection. I was in incredible pain and trying my best to learn how to be a new mum, while recovering from major surgery. After a couple of months, as the wound began to heal, I started developing some other nasty symptoms – bleeding when I went to the bathroom. The invasive surgery had triggered a reaction in my body – an autoimmune disease called ulcerative colitis. The doctors wanted to be sure of the diagnosis before they medicated me for the condition, so a colonoscopy was scheduled. I had to wait six weeks. Six weeks of agonizing pain – much worse than the original surgery. I was in so much distress, I was suicidal. The only thing that stopped me was my baby, Arthur. He needed me. My parents flew out to live with us for two months. I just couldn't cope with a baby while my husband was working. I wasn't even allowed to lift him.

The colonoscopy confirmed that I did have ulcerative colitis, and after some trial and error with medications, I finally found one that worked. Within just one week of taking the medication, I was in remission. The relief was palpable and the absence of pain was euphoric. I returned to the UK shortly after. It was lovely to be home and surrounded by friends and family. The trauma became less and life moved on, as it always does. But something had changed. I was scared. Scared of everything. I'd come so close to my own mortality that I became obsessed with it. I didn't want to even leave the house for fear of what might happen to me or my son. What did I do to cope with this anxiety? I started to drink wine again. When I drank, I was capable of going out. I wasn't as scared. My anxiety ebbed away and I could live life like a semi-normal person. Alcohol became crucial for me to have any sort of a social life. I was lost without it.

When my second son, Alfie, came along, I had an entirely different experience. He was so eager to get out into the world that he came along almost two months early. The doctors had planned for me to have a caesarean a month early. (Because of my previous scarring, I wasn't allowed to deliver naturally.) But I ended up having another emergency caesarean because I'd gone into pre-term labour. Despite being born so early, Alfie was in perfect health. Born at five pounds five ounces, he was like a tiny little doll. He never cried, slept all the time and, for the most part, I didn't even know I had a second baby! Compared to my first experience of motherhood, it was a breeze. Nonetheless, when I finished breastfeeding, I quickly returned to my ole faithful, Pinot Grigio. Juggling two children under five was hard work, and I hadn't anticipated just how much more challenging two children would be than one!

Society has long recognized that raising children is a tough, exhausting and relentless task. In the 60s and 70s, Valium (the brand name for the prescription drug diazepam) was prescribed by GPs to stressed-out housewives, affectionately known as "mother's little helper". Valium is now far less socially acceptable, and doctors are very reluctant to prescribe it because it's highly addictive. However, alcohol, which is a far more harmful and damaging drug, is positively promoted on a global scale.

Mums are an easy target for alcohol advertising. When I was drinking, I was in a perpetual cycle of guilt and self-hatred. I felt guilty when I was working because my boys weren't getting my attention. I felt like I was useless at my job because I was always mentally planning the never-ending to-do list for when I got home. I was so stressed and anxious trying to balance everything. As much as I'm embarrassed to admit it, from the moment I finished work, I just saw every evening as something to navigate as quickly as possible. I would get my kids into bed at the speed of lightning, so I could finally switch off my brain and knock back my wine in peace. Any suggestion of a drink, by any source, was welcome.

Undoubtedly, there have been many wonderful changes in recent years that support mothers and recognize the need for a work-life balance, enabling more women to manage a professional life alongside caring for children. Flexible working, breastfeeding rooms at the office, and positive action campaigns to recruit women into senior roles are all examples of an increasingly supportive and inclusive society that favours working mothers.

However, what isn't often discussed is the sheer difficulty of "having it all" (modern values and inclusion aside). We live in a world where we're taught that we can do anything and become anyone we choose to be. While this is undoubtedly an exciting time to be alive, playing devil's advocate, if everything is accessible, and we really can have it all, then why is our mental health (on a global scale) in such rapid decline?

What I mean by this, is that having everything – working, becoming successful and raising a family – is a massive responsibility that takes an enormous amount of time, effort and energy. We're being raised in an era of "everything is possible", but how much work and stress does it take to actually achieve this? A lot! Especially with the constant demands incoming from modern technology.

Our world is developing and changing at a breakneck pace. Look at how technology has transformed over the last 20 years. I was raised during a time when getting online involved dial-up (and mostly a lot of waiting around and noise), reading at the library, shopping in actual stores, and my most significant technological achievement was keeping a Tamagotchi pet alive.

Now, I wake up to a barrage of emails (work and personal), messages (work and personal), endless social media notifications and newsfeeds. My brain deals with more information before eight in the morning on a single day than it used to deal with in an entire week. No wonder we're all bloody stressed! Put simply, our planet has evolved far more quickly than our minds. We are not designed to exist in the world we currently live in, and technology will inevitably continue to advance far more rapidly than we can cope with.

So, how do we manage in a world that is much more advanced than we have evolved to deal with, while also raising children? We turn to alcohol. We use it to block out the constant information and noise that cause tension and stress. Who can blame us? It feels almost essential for modern survival. We're not constructed to live in the modern world, so we need an antidote to the symptoms it causes, and alcohol provides a quick, almost instantaneous fix. When I was drinking, I'd welcome a minor car crash to get a broken limb, just so I could rest in the hospital and have my food brought to me. In this fantasy, I would be incapable of looking after children and would have nothing to do except scroll through my phone and furiously masturbate (one of the many activities I never normally have time for).

Wine, for me, felt like an essential crutch to shake off the workday and improve the weekend. How, as an entire society, have we been brainwashed into believing that being intoxicated is a necessary component of parenting? Moreover, we think it's actually funny. Personally, I think it's easier to accept the notion that it's amusing when mums finally get some child-free time and go wild (*Bad Moms* the movie is a good example) rather than acknowledging that we're so stressed, burned out and mentally struggling that we're all simply addicted to a very dangerous drug we've consumed simply to cope with busy life. And if we're all doing it, it can't really be a problem, right?

Jokes about "mummy needing wine" to deal with kids are not funny. Society endorses drunken motherhood in particular by labelling it as hilarious – just look at the gift card section in the supermarket; how many of them relate to mums needing wine? It's pretty grim. We need a change. We need to support our mothers to be able to work and raise a family in a healthy and sustainable way.

Think of it this way – would you have any sympathy for a mother addicted to heroin whose child died in the night because she was in a comatose state and didn't hear them fall down the stairs? How many times have I put my children to bed and then drunk more than a bottle of wine? Before I quit, most nights, if I'm honest. Would I have heard either of them fall down the stairs? I sincerely doubt it. At the time, I didn't even consider that this wasn't a safe way to parent. As far as I was concerned, alcohol was the *antidote* to parental stress.

So, what is the secret to quitting alcohol and handling parenting like a pro? There is none. Drinking alcohol makes it so much harder! Quitting drinking makes motherhood so much easier! That's it. Believe me. Just think about the lengths you go to in order to sustain a life involving drinking, and I promise, quitting is going to feel like giving up a low-paid, shit job for a life of ease and luxury by comparison.

If you are a daily drinker, you have already developed amazing resilience, grit and determination – you're just applying it to the wrong things. From the moment you wake up, you are on the back-burner. Hungover, tired from a restless night of poor sleep and night anxiety, dehydrated, grumpy, feeling like shit, your head is banging, and then you wake up to the sound of screaming children. No wonder you start the day wishing it were five in the afternoon! From the moment you wake up, you have to battle through your busy day, all while trying not to vomit. Kudos! If you're an addict, you're probably the most resilient person you know.

Getting the kids ready for school is probably my least favourite job on the planet. Correction. It was. I used to snooze my alarm clock until the last available second, drag myself downstairs and basically throw breakfast together and repeat myself over and over, telling the kids to get ready, until I found myself screaming at them and running out of the door in my gym kit, so I could at least create the illusion of being an amazing mother who drops her kids off at school and then goes for a workout – as opposed to being hungover as fuck with no time to shower.

I would walk out of the school gates feeling like I had already been through a rough day, before rushing home to log on for work and then trying to sort out my bomb tip of a house in between meetings, all the while feeling like total shit. If you start your mornings like I did, then, like I said, you already have an amazing skill – resilience. If you can get your body into a state where your kidneys are screaming, your head is falling apart and still get your kids to school on time, just imagine how much more you could achieve sober? "High-functioning alcoholic" is really just a term used to describe incredible productivity in spite of an alcohol abuse problem. Just imagine how high-functioning you could be when permanently sober? You'll practically have a superpower!

Since I've been sober, I tend to wake up at six. Turns out, I am more of a morning person than I realized! I often get up and make American pancakes before my kids are even out of bed. I make sure their school stuff is organized the night before, so that after breakfast, I can help them get dressed instead of screaming at them to do it while I get on with other things. I talk to them about what their day might look like and what we can do when they get home from school. We generally leave the house with no shouting and no drama. When I drop my kids off at their classrooms, every day I tell them I love them, I will miss them, and I can't wait to see them later – because I mean it.

Of course, my kids still have moments when I want to scream into a cushion. Like the days where Alfie's socks "don't fit perfectly" – then I'm in for a shit show of a morning, even without a hangover. I said giving up alcohol makes parenting easier; it's not fucking magic. But now I genuinely want to spend time with them, sock issues aside.

I avoided my children to avoid stress. I've come to see that it's the avoidance that causes most of the strain in the first place. My children (all children, for that matter) only really want two things: love and attention. Once they have both of these things, they are fulfilled and content. When my boys are happy, I'm happy. I have a go-to method for reducing the stress of mothering that works better than anything else I've tried – I just play with them. It doesn't matter if it's a short period of time. Even if I only play a game with them for ten minutes, my stress levels reduce significantly, because they are happier. The best thing about this is that giving my boys my undivided attention for a short time makes an infinite difference to their overall behaviour. It's a fantastic bargaining chip. "I will play with you now, but then I have to cook dinner and do the laundry, and you need to be good and let me get on with it."

Kids are desperate for our attention – even if it's negative. If we give them attention in the first place, they tend to be a lot less demanding. Think about how much time you really engage and play with your kids. When I was drinking, I avoided play time at all costs. I didn't realize how much I could benefit – not just because my boys behave better when they've got my attention, but because I also feel better when I'm living in the moment. When I was newly sober and the boys were stressing me out, I made a conscious decision to divert my attention to them when the craving for wine smacked me around the face at 5 p.m. every afternoon. Jigsaws, board games, trips to the park, crafting, baking – I got stuck into anything that would serve as a distraction. It really is a tonic (minus the gin!). Getting off my phone and social media also massively helped to combat the constant influx of the stress hormone (cortisol) to my brain with the endless stream of notifications coming through. Remember, we're not designed to live like this. When we put our phones down, we live in the moment, as the universe intended.

I am happily sober and proud that my children are young enough that they won't remember me ever having a glass of wine in my hand because I'm far too busy having fun with them for that. Do you question if you can parent without alcohol? If you've ever done the school run on a hangover, then trust me, you can do sober parenting with your eyes shut! It's so much easier. Of course, being sober can be tough at times – life isn't always easy, especially when it comes to being a mum – but I promise you this: living life addicted to alcohol is ten times harder.

Mum Guilt

"Guilt is a useless feeling. It's never enough to make you change direction, only enough to make you useless."

Daniel Nayeri

I am such a lucky mum. I've got the best two boys I could ever wish for. It's so fascinating to me that I can be raising two boys, using exactly the same parenting techniques, but who are such completely different little personalities. Arthur is my eldest. He is nine going on 60. An old soul. Deeply thoughtful, empathetic, desperately sweet and affectionate. He is an absolute stickler for "rules" and I've never met anyone with such a solid moral compass for doing the right thing at all costs. Alfie, on the other hand, at six years old, is a little firecracker. Enigmatic, fiercely brave, a perpetual joker and with a laugh so infectious, anyone within earshot ends up in giggles. Super cheeky and absolutely going to be lifelong trouble.

I love my boys more than life – but my God, those two little creatures are the mother of all time-suckers! They're hard work. It often feels that there are never enough hours in the day.

I honestly have no idea how anyone manages with more than two kids. I have the utmost admiration for the mamas that do – and if you fall into this category, I'd love to know your secret for how the hell you cope!

One of the most common concerns I hear from mums is that they never have enough time to do anything for themselves. Some don't even recognize that they do nothing for themselves at all! All of their time is taken up with daily mum tasks – the relentless daily grind of school runs, cooking, driving to various extra-curricular classes, cleaning, tidying, soft play, children's parties, trips to the park and so on. They do countless activities, none of which are enjoyable for themselves. In actuality, it's not that mums have no time; it's just that they prioritize everything and everyone else over and above themselves.

When you get on a flight, you're always told to put your own oxygen mask on before you assist anyone else – including your children. Why? Because if you pass out, you can't help your children. Similarly, if you don't take care of yourself and your needs, how can you possibly expect to look after anyone else?

So why is it that mums tend to put their children and everything else before themselves? Mum guilt. That's why. We see countless representations on social media about what it takes to be a great mum, and that standard is generally perfection. What we forget is that people only post snapshots of the good stuff. For example, you might see a perfect photo of a family dressed up for Halloween. All the costumes look amazing, and the make-up looks like it's been done professionally. Everyone is grinning manically and looking so bloody happy. Why didn't you make that much effort? Why didn't you go "all out" with the costumes and make-up? Are you not as good as the other mums? Are you failing your children because you're not giving them the same experiences?

We question ourselves, doubt our parenting and worry we're not doing enough. We mentally beat ourselves up for being terrible at "mumming" and then we try harder. Our already busy schedules get overloaded with more crap so that we don't feel like we're failing our children. It's mum guilt at its worst. And you know what? It's all bullshit!

The Halloween photo is just a single-second snapshot. It doesn't show that the mum has been working all week, busting her backside to get these costumes prepared because she feels guilty about not spending enough time with her children. She hasn't been able to see the kids all week and has been home too late from work every day to put them to bed. You don't see the two hours of screaming from the kids who don't like having the make-up applied and keep whining that it's "itchy". You don't see the children kicking off because the costume doesn't fit just right, throwing a tantrum and declaring they're "not going" trick-or-treating unless they can get a new costume. You don't see the mum tearing her hair out, desperately trying to placate her brood and get them ready in time, simultaneously shouting at her children for being ungrateful little buggers. You only see the one-second snapshot – the end result. The single perfect moment. This mum likely posted the picture to feel better about her own mum guilt, to get validation for her efforts, to get praise, to feel happier, to feel better about her own relentless struggle.

It's so easy to look at social media and conclude that you're not enough. But you are. You may have skipped Halloween this year. You may have been too busy. Who cares? Dropping some things is essential to living a balanced life. We can't do everything. And when we try, we lose valuable time, and all sense of ourselves.

The problem with striving for perfection is that we become perpetually burned out, tired, exhausted and miserable. We forget that being a mum is something we do. It's part of our life. But it doesn't define who we are. Before you had children, you had time for yourself in abundance. You did what you wanted, when you wanted to do it. First and foremost, you are a person. You are a person and you deserve to have a life for yourself, as well as giving one to your children. When you give up everything you know and love, to make as much time as possible to dedicate to your children, it's easy to lose your own identity – what makes you *you*. It's not selfish to have time out for yourself. It's essential. When you take care of your own needs first, you are able to show up for your family from a place of happiness. Only once you put your own mask on can you look after anyone else.

Mum guilt made my life completely miserable. No matter how hard I tried, I never felt like I was doing enough. Now that I prioritize my own needs, I feel better about being a mum – because I'm happier in my own skin. Above all, my children need a happy mum because they can sense when I'm miserable or exhausted. I'm a better mum when I take care of myself. You can start to prioritize yourself in various ways. One of the things I do every day is to make myself a coffee before tending to my boys. As soon as I get up, I'm inevitably met with a barrage of requests.

"Mummy, can I have... Mummy, I need... Mummy, I want..."

My response is always the same.

"Be patient, darling. I'll be with you once I've made myself a coffee."

If I don't do this, I will NEVER get to make myself a coffee! If I don't slow down and actively take this stance, the list of requests never ends, and I never stop. My children are not hard done by having to wait an extra two minutes for me to make their breakfast. It won't kill them! They know they won't get a damn thing out of me until I have a coffee in hand. This is a simple example, but it can be applied throughout the day and helps begin a significant shift in mindset towards prioritizing your own needs.

So, what does "mum guilt" have to do with quitting alcohol? It's one of the reasons that so many mums drink in the first place. Most of the clients I have worked with have spent their entire time as a mother putting everyone else first. Their entire life is the daily grind – one mum task after another. They've lost a sense of who they are. They don't do things they enjoy just for themselves – they're unhappy and often deeply miserable. Alcohol gives an instant dopamine hit – artificial happiness. It certainly did for me. I would run myself ragged trying to be the best mum possible, and at the end of each day, I just wanted to shut off, relax, wind down, do nothing and block out every negative emotion I had. Forget about my shitty life (as I then saw it).

I used to spend an extraordinary amount of time taking on unnecessary tasks. For instance, emails from the school continually flood into my inbox like an ongoing game of Tetris. As soon as I delete one, a new email appears. I used to think of these requests as mandatory, because I simply felt like a bad mum for saying "no". Now, I am selective about what I say "yes" to. For example, the school might make a request to parents to bring cakes in for a bake sale. I have three choices: add "baking cakes" to my already ridiculous schedule, buy some from the shop, or just delete that stupid, sodding email. I'll go with the latter, thank you. If I didn't work full-time and run a business, I would happily do this. I enjoy baking. What I don't like is having to bake on demand when I already have a hectic schedule. I don't want to do it. So, I don't. This doesn't make me a bad mum. It makes me a busy one. I'd love to have the time and energy to help out at the school more, but I don't. This is just one of the areas in my life that I have to be "less than" in order to maintain my overall sanity.

Mum guilt is a very real thing, and it's something that many of us experience at some point in our lives. It's that nagging feeling that we're not doing enough, that we're not measuring up to some imaginary standard that we've set for ourselves – or that is set by social media. And one of the sure-fire ways to know if you're suffering from mum guilt is the use of the word "should".

Think about it. How many times a day do you say to yourself, "I should be doing this", or "I should have done that"? When we use the word "should", we're imposing a standard on ourselves that is often unrealistic and unattainable. We compare ourselves to others and create our own impossible standards. But here's the thing: the only person who is saying "should" is you. No one is forcing you to do anything that you don't want to do, other than you! No one else is judging you as harshly as you are judging yourself. And the truth is, you're doing the best you can with what you have. You're a mum for crying out loud! You're juggling a million different things at once and keeping small people alive. You're allowed a rest too!

So, the next time you catch yourself saying "should", try to reframe it. Instead of saying, "I should be doing more," try saying, "I'm doing the best I can right now." Instead of comparing yourself to other mums who seem to have it all together, remember that everyone has their own struggles and challenges. No one really knows what's going on behind closed doors. Everyone has an issue of some sort going on. A hidden battle we're unaware of.

And above all, remember to give yourself a break. You're doing an amazing job, and you deserve to feel proud of yourself. I'll end the chapter with this one thought: when you're enjoying your life and doing some of the things that you want to do just for yourself, you don't want to block out the world – you want to live in it.

The Power of Yes and the Power of No

The power of no

> "Saying no can be the ultimate self-care."

Claudia Black

I have spent most of my life to date as a people pleaser. I spent pretty much my entire twenties and thirties desperately trying to ensure that other people would like me. I couldn't bear the thought of someone disliking me, let alone hating me. I held a deep-rooted fear of not being likeable or lovable, so I spent 20 years trying to curate a personality that would please everyone. I rarely said no to anyone. I said yes to taking on additional work, even when I didn't have time. I agreed to nights out to places that really didn't interest me. If I was going out for dinner with someone and they asked where I wanted to go, I would always say, "Oh, I don't mind at all! You choose!" I didn't consider my wants or needs. I just went along with what everyone else wanted because I was scared. I was scared of not being liked, not fitting in, losing friendships and being alone.

Since becoming sober (and after lots of therapy), I've learned that my deep-rooted insecurities prevented me from finding my own voice. I've been on a journey to find out who I am, what I want, and what I need for myself to be happy. If I'm going to live authentically and be myself, it's imperative that sometimes I say no to people.

I couldn't say no to people when I was a drinker because alcohol kept me firmly rooted in my insecurities. I hated myself. If I said no to people, and they hated me too, that would have been too much to cope with. Now that I'm sober, I've grown to love who I am. Alcohol caused me to say and do things that weren't congruent with my sober values – I felt awful about the person I was, and I couldn't be confident to assert what I wanted or needed because I didn't feel worthy of that.

When you say no to things that you don't want to do, it frees up your time to say yes to the stuff that you really do want to do. "Mumming" is a very busy sport! We don't get much free time, and it's precious. If you spend your time doing things that don't interest you just to please others, you take something away from yourself – the chance to enjoy your life the way you want to.

The word no carries significant power, as it signifies the boundaries we set for ourselves. Although some people may not like our boundaries, it is essential that they respect them, regardless of whether they agree with them. If they do not, we have the right to dismiss them. I now say no to anything that

I do not want to do, except when it may adversely affect someone I care about. For instance, if a friend invited me to a concert, and I did not like the band, I would politely decline and explain that it was not my kind of music. However, if the same friend asked me to attend the concert because she had gone through a break-up and needed company, I would go to support her. Being there for people I love is crucial to my own values.

Have you ever found yourself saying yes when you meant no? Take some time to ponder this. Can you say no more often? Saying no can be empowering and liberating. Give it a try! You've nothing to lose and so much to gain. When you choose to say no to the things you don't want to do, you free your time to explore how you really want to live your life. You give yourself the possibility of saying yes to new opportunities that excite you. And herein lies a whole new way of living and exploring your authentic self.

The power of yes

"Say no to new adventures."

Said no one. Ever.

I first discovered the power of yes when I read *Yes Man*, a book written by Danny Wallace. Although it was turned into a film starring Jim Carrey, I highly recommend reading the book if you haven't already – it's way better. It's a true story about a man who decides to say yes to everything for one year. The book is highly amusing, and the experiment yields some incredible results, but the primary takeaway is that saying yes opens up endless possibilities and opportunities in life.

The power of no allows us to stop doing things we do not want to do. Conversely, the power of yes enables us to do the things we would like to do and explore activities we would never have considered before. It also allows us to try things we might find terrifying, by simply saying, "Why not? Fuck it! I'll give it a go!" If you are a drinker, you are probably familiar with the power of yes as it often goes hand in hand with drinking too much alcohol. Alcohol consumption diminishes our inhibitions, and we end up agreeing to do things we would not consider when sober – often with dangerous consequences. I always became a "yes woman" after a few drinks. I made so many poor decisions with my inhibitions lowered. Conversely, saying yes while sober is both safe and fun.

As I mentioned earlier, one of the reasons I was afraid of quitting alcohol was that I thought I would lose my fun side. I used to believe that alcohol made me more entertaining and that I would never agree to do many of the things I did when I was drunk. However, it turns out that I am just as much fun, if not more so, now that I am sober. This is because I have embraced the power of yes. The danger with saying yes while drinking is that you may not appreciate the risks involved. In contrast, when you are sober and say yes to something terrifying, such as skydiving, the experience can be even more amazing because you feel the fear and do it anyway. The fear itself is what makes the experience so exhilarating. You get an adrenaline rush, but you are also safe. When you are sober, your brain is on your side, and it is there to protect you. When you drink, your senses are dulled, and while drinking may numb unwanted emotions, it can also squash all positive feelings as well.

When I'm asked to do something that sounds fun, I automatically ask myself, "Why not?" If it's not an outright no, it's a potential yes. If the only reason not to do something is that I'm scared, I'm sure as hell going to do it anyway. This is how I began to find fun again in sobriety: by saying yes to any possibility, opportunity and new experience that could be enjoyable. When we take that leap of faith and say yes, we discover new parts of ourselves and uncover hidden strengths and abilities. Saying yes can also lead to unexpected connections and relationships, as we meet new people and form bonds over shared experiences. Ultimately, saying yes allows us to live a richer and more fulfilling life, one that is full of adventure, discovery and joy.

The next time someone asks you to do something that you haven't tried or that scares you, and it's not an outright no for you, ask yourself, "Why not?" A potential yes is the start of a new adventure. Where could it take you? I have no idea – but it sounds like it could be fun to me.

Why Is it so Hard to Find Out How to Quit?

"Sometimes the questions are complicated and the answers are simple."

Dr Seuss

There are numerous books about addiction and recovery. I believe I read most of them during my early quest to quit drinking. However, the issue with the majority of literature about quitting alcohol is that, while there is a vast amount of information available on what alcohol is and what it does, there is very little guidance on how to get sober and, more importantly, stay sober. Many successful books focus on unravelling the myths surrounding alcohol, with the premise that once you understand its harmful effects, you'll no longer crave it. While I agree that understanding the nature of alcohol is a crucial component of recovery, I believe it only accounts for 10 per cent of the solution. The other 90 per cent involves sorting out your life and learning how to cope without the crutch of alcohol.

Despite reading an excessive amount of "quit lit", I still felt clueless about how to navigate life sober. Alcohol had been my go-to solution for every problem I faced. Without it, what could I use to de-stress after a hectic day at work? How would I cope with a major setback? I yearned for someone to tell me what to do and when to do it.

The first programme I tried was hypnotherapy-based. I chose this option during the time when I wanted to cut down on drinking but wasn't ready to consider sobriety as a life choice. The course was advertised as a successful method to control drinking, which greatly appealed to me at the time. If I could just stop after one or two drinks, all my problems would go away. I wouldn't have to worry about getting drunk, saying or doing stupid things, and my health wouldn't be at risk. I purchased the hypnotherapy course because it promised an easy fix, a lie that I desperately wanted to believe. I thought controlling my alcohol consumption was possible. Obviously, it wasn't. I felt hugely disappointed when I signed up for the programme. I received a link to a 30-minute audio recording with instructions to listen to the same recording every night for 30 days. It was essentially just a man speaking in very slow, dulcet tones and talking about visualizing a situation where you only have one drink and feel happy to stop there. That was it. I bought the programme because the reviews were good, but I have no idea where these positive reviews came from. I can't imagine anyone using this programme and feeling anything other than deep disappointment. The only benefit I gained from the audio recording was that after multiple nights of listening to the same thing over and over, it was boring enough to put me to sleep.

There are many people who can moderate their alcohol intake, but I am not one of them. No course on earth can change that. I am now content with the fact that I can't moderate, and I don't want to be someone who can. Moderation always carries the risk of a worsening problem. As I've already mentioned, my dad is a good example of this. He has been a lifetime moderator, but when my mum died, he became a heavy drinker within a few short weeks, consuming three bottles of red wine a night.

Once I accepted that moderation was well and truly off the cards for me, I desperately researched recovery courses. There are loads of online programmes that claim to get you sober quickly, and it seemed as good a place to start as any. I tried a few, but none of them were successful. Now that I'm sober, I understand why. The first one I tried was a 30-day online programme that claimed to help you get sober quickly and easily. All of the content was about why alcohol is bad and why sobriety is good, which was great, but it didn't offer me anything that I hadn't already read in the many books I'd already devoured. Additionally, it finished right at the time when I was entering boredom-ville. I had no happy hormones and felt flat and miserable, so it wasn't exactly the best time to finish a programme. I didn't even feel like a human being yet. Now that I know it takes up to 90 days for dopamine levels to return to normal, it doesn't make any sense to use any programme that takes less time than this to complete. You essentially finish when you need the most help and support, and this particular course didn't offer any support other than information about alcohol. There was zero accountability, and I couldn't ask anyone for advice. I had so many questions but no answers.

Before I started reading quit literature, I considered Alcoholics Anonymous (AA). However, I quickly changed my mind after being surprised by the number of negative comments I read about the AA recovery programme, most of which were contained within well-established quit literature. AA has been around for so long and has been widely hailed as the go-to method for quitting worldwide. It has become such an unstoppable beast that, much like alcohol, it is not questioned. If you tell anyone you are an alcoholic, nine times out of ten, they will suggest you go to AA – not because they know anything about it or how successful it is, but because it's such a giant organization, everyone has heard of it, and nothing has superseded its existence on the same scale since it first began, in 1935.

I first started to challenge my beliefs about AA when I read *Quit Like a Woman* by Holly Whitaker – a fantastic book that I still pick up to reread every now and then. Whitaker explains a great deal about the history of AA and, in particular, why it doesn't work for women because it was designed exclusively for men by men. When AA began, women weren't allowed to attend meetings – they weren't even considered capable of becoming alcoholics! Whitaker explores drinking culture with a feminist outlook, explaining and dismantling AA's foundations at great length – I thoroughly recommend this book to anyone who wants to learn more about why male-centric recovery programmes do not work for women.

After reading Whitaker's thoughts on AA, I became fascinated about the organization and conducted some research of my own. AA was founded by Bill Wilson in 1935. The 12-step programme is a faith-based approach centred around surrendering to God, accepting that you have no power or control over alcohol, and taking various steps to own your failures and make amends with people whom you have "wronged" while drinking.

Bill Wilson quit drinking but remained a heavy smoker, which is a big red flag for me. The man who created a programme to quit drinking swapped one addiction for another and used smoking as a coping mechanism. If his method is so amazing, why did he need an equally unhealthy crutch to deal with his life? Bill Wilson was so reliant on nicotine that he continued to smoke on his deathbed, even after being diagnosed with emphysema and pneumonia and hooked up to an oxygen tank to help him breathe. During his final days, he asked his nurse for whisky on four separate occasions. I have not found any information that documents whether or not his requests were honoured.

Now, some might argue that on your deathbed, it makes little difference whether or not you have a few shots of hard liquor. However, one hard fact cannot be ignored: Bill Wilson did not lose the desire to drink. He spent many years in recovery but never lost the craving. This makes perfect sense when you look at the teachings of the AA programme. One of the mantras frequently used is "one day at a time". Why is this used? The AA theory is that once you accept that you're powerless over alcohol and an alcoholic, you will always be an alcoholic. You're "diseased", after all. "One day at a time" is used to lessen the blow. Getting through one day is easier than envisaging getting through a lifetime and some people find this mantra helpful to get them through a moment of craving. I don't find it helpful at all. If you announce yourself as an alcoholic in AA, you will forever be doomed to wander the planet "one day at a time" because you will always be at risk of relapse. Depressing, isn't it? Sobriety does not sound at all appealing when using this mantra.

AA works on the premise of the disease model of addiction theory. Essentially, most people are okay to drink alcohol and are able to moderate, but some of us are unfortunate to have been born "diseased" with some sort of genetic component that means we are effectively allergic to alcohol and can't be trusted with it. I'll agree that I can't be trusted with alcohol, but I'm certainly no more diseased than anyone else who chooses to consume it. If you are somehow predisposed to have a problem with alcohol, but you never touch a drink, you cannot by definition be an alcoholic because you'll never know. How does the disease model of addiction theory apply to people like my dad? He was a proven moderator over several decades, who suddenly developed a three-bottle-of-wine-a-day habit after the death of my mother. How would AA view that? Was he always diseased? Did the disease lie dormant and sneak up on him in later life? Or was he just a man who was able to control his drinking, until he wasn't?

The disease model is inherently flawed. Clearly, some people are more prone to addiction than others. From the second I tried alcohol, I was hooked. I always got more drunk than my friends. I knew I was "different" in that regard. This doesn't change the fact that anyone on the planet can become an alcoholic if they consume too much of the stuff. That's not a disease. It's a predictable, biological reaction of the human body. Drink a lot, and your tolerance will increase. Drink enough, and you'll eventually become physically dependent. Keep going hard enough, and it will eventually kill you.

When I read about the disease model theory, I hypothesized about an experiment that would prove that anyone is capable of becoming addicted to alcohol. Imagine if there were a study in which they used a group of moderate drinkers, or better still, people who had never tried alcohol before. During the experiment, they would give each person a small amount of alcohol to drink each day. Every day, the amount would be increased until eventually, the group was consuming the equivalent of two bottles of wine every day. After a few months, the programme would conclude, and the group would be free to stop drinking as soon as they left the experiment. Do you think any of them would be able to just stop? Obviously, this would be a rather unhealthy and dangerous experiment, and I'm pretty certain there wouldn't be many volunteers. But just think about it with a common-sense approach – if someone is regularly ingesting alcohol, they will become physically dependent, whether or not they enjoy it. If anyone is capable of becoming dependent, doesn't it follow that we all must be "diseased"?

American psychiatrist Lance Dodes, in *The Sober Truth*, says that research indicates that only 5 to 8 per cent of the people who go to one or more AA meetings achieve sobriety. This study has attracted some controversy, but if a doctor told you that you had between a 5 per cent and 8 per cent chance of survival, you'd be pretty bummed. If you were going to invest some money in a company, and they told you that only 5 per cent to 8 per cent of their clients made money, would you invest? It's a staggeringly low figure of success for the biggest addiction recovery organization in the world. So why is it so low? I believe it's because the theories of AA are not based on science, or even facts. They're based on shame.

I've paraphrased the 12 steps of AA for simplicity:

1. *The 12-step process begins with an admission that you are powerless over drugs or alcohol.*
2. *Covet the belief that a Higher Power greater than yourself can fix you.*
3. *Make a decision to turn your will and your life over to God.*
4. *Make a comprehensive list of all the awful things you've ever said and done.*
5. *Admit all of the above to God, yourself and another human being.*
6. *Decide you'd like God to remove all your defects.*
7. *Now ask God to remove your defects.*
8. *Make a list of all the people you've ever hurt and decide that you're going to apologize and make amends to all of them.*
9. *Now go and apologize.*
10. *Continue to write down whenever you've fucked up and keep apologizing for it.*
11. *Pray to God and ask for his will for us to be carried out.*

*12. Have an epiphany/spiritual awakening as the result of the
above steps and continue to practise them forever more.*

I think I can sum up the 12 steps with this statement: "You're
the problem. Feel really bad about this. Apologize a lot. Pray on
it."

Just reading the 12 steps was enough of a deterrent to stop
me from walking into an AA meeting when I first decided to
quit alcohol. I already knew that I was a total fuck-up. I didn't
need to feel any more shame. I had enough to last me a lifetime.
My self-esteem was at an all-time low. Focusing on the damage
I'd caused to myself and others was not the answer for me. If
people could quit by simply focusing on the negatives caused by
alcohol, no one would drink. We all know about the damage.
When we drink too much and want to stop, we live in disgrace
every single day. Every night, we wake up with constant worries
about our health and fears for the future. If shame was the
answer to quitting, I would have managed it many years ago.

If surrendering to God and feeling ashamed isn't the answer,
why does AA work for some people? I personally believe that the
12 steps have little to do with any success resulting from AA.
How can they? How can focusing on being humble, making
amends and surrendering to God be the answer to a physiological
addiction and learning to cope with life while sober? Firstly, if
you are religious, I'm sure you will have already prayed to get
sober on many occasions before. And no doubt, you already feel
terrible about yourself. So, what's new? What is there within the
12 steps that tells you anything that you didn't already know?

I decided to attend some AA meetings after many months of sobriety to satisfy my own curiosity, to see how it works, and to challenge my own opinions, which were based entirely on research. It wasn't for me, and the 12 steps remain elusive to me, but I found the experience interesting and met some lovely people. I personally believe that any success resulting from AA is due to the sense of community, accountability and having a sponsor. When we try to quit alone, we only let ourselves down if we fail, and this is why using willpower alone is rarely successful. Having a tribe of people wrapped around you is crucial.

I didn't like AA because the theories just don't make sense to me and I wanted to connect with people whom I could relate to – not just about alcohol, but life in general. I am a woman and a mother. I wanted to talk to other women going through the same struggles as I was, and the group I went to predominantly consisted of men. I wanted to talk to mums who understood what it's like to get back from the school run and be counting down the minutes until it was socially acceptable to open a bottle of wine. I wanted to connect with mums who understood how challenging it was to deal with temper tantrums and who would understand how scared I was about never having fun again as a sober woman. Maybe if I had continued to go to AA, I would have eventually found someone with whom I connected; maybe not. I wanted to seek out a whole tribe of women in the same boat, and I found my tribe on Facebook. There are countless online support groups. You just have to look for the ones that resonate with you. I chose groups full of mums who connected with my struggle.

In these groups I was able to read about other women going through the exact same challenges that I was. It didn't matter to me that I couldn't meet these women in person. There were stories of mums with cirrhosis. I felt grateful I wasn't at that point. There were stories of women who had many years sober. They were inspiring. There were stories of mums in the exact same situation as me. I felt understood. The only thing that was missing from the online groups was accountability. So, having read Claire Pooley's *The Sober Diaries*, I decided to follow in her footsteps and start a blog. I told myself that if I wrote a blog and even had a few followers, I would be accountable to them. If my words resonated with other people and helped them to stay sober, I couldn't let them down by relapsing. The longer that time went on, the more followers I amassed, the more comments I received about inspiring others, the more it spurred me on to keep going.

I have no doubt that there will be women reading this book who have used AA and become sober. More power to any of you in this boat, or anyone who wants to try it. The method clearly does work for some people and I'm not trying to bash the process for the sake of it. I can imagine that if you're deeply religious, or you like the idea of face-to-face group meetings, this may be a process that completely resonates with you. What I want to get across to you is that AA is just one of the methods of quitting. It's not the only one. There are so many different approaches to achieving sobriety. The key is finding a method that speaks to you. And that choice is yours.

How to Quit

Winston Churchill

My secret to achieving sobriety is straightforward: 10 per cent education, 90 per cent life organization. The education component involves learning about alcohol, the harmful effects of consuming it, and dismantling any notion that it has any redeeming qualities. I strongly recommend reading a lot of "quit lit", listening to podcasts, and participating in online support groups – any or all of it, if it helps you. Once you no longer view alcohol as having any value, the urge to drink fades away.

The remaining 90 per cent is where the real work lies. Alcohol is not the root issue, but rather a coping mechanism for a deeper problem. However, identifying that problem can be challenging as it is often hidden, muddled or entirely elusive. When alcohol becomes a significant issue, it can further complicate the process of discovering what is truly wrong. For me, I struggled with an internal voice that I was trying to quiet, and alcohol seemed like the perfect solution. But when I became sober, that voice became louder and louder until it was screaming, and I couldn't ignore my underlying insecurities any longer. It was as if I was a teenager trapped in an adult's body, as I had started drinking at a young age to cope with my problems, and never truly learned how to deal with them. I was 39 years old with the emotional intelligence of a 14-year-old. What the fuck?!

Sorting out my life was not an easy task, but having a plan and sticking to it made it more manageable. I realized that I needed help, and sought out support from others who had been in a similar situation. Through this process, I was able to learn the necessary skills to mature emotionally and deal with my problems without relying on alcohol. So, my advice to anyone seeking sobriety is to educate yourself on alcohol and prioritize getting your ducks in a row – it's the key to long-term success.

When I made the decision to quit drinking, I found that the existing systems, programmes and methods just didn't work or resonate with me. So, I decided to take matters into my own hands and create my own system. I began by utilizing my knowledge of alcohol and the timeline of what happens when you quit. I then took action on each of these areas as I experienced the different physical and emotional states that come with quitting.

This personalized approach allowed me to tailor my journey to my specific needs, ensuring that I was addressing my unique challenges and weaknesses. It was a trial-and-error process, but over time, I found what worked for me and what didn't. This is how I achieved long-term sobriety – by developing a plan that was centred on my needs as a woman and as a mum. I now use the programme I developed to help other mums achieve sobriety – because I understand the unique challenges and I've been through the same journey and come out the other side not just sober, but sober and with zero desire to drink again. I don't navigate life "one day at a time". I no longer see any value in drinking. I'm free.

I believe that everyone has their own path to sobriety, and what works for one person may not work for another. Therefore, it's essential to take the time to figure out what approach will be the most effective for you. This may require some experimentation, but the effort is worth it. With a plan that is tailored to your specific situation, you will be more equipped to deal with the challenges that come with quitting and achieve lasting success.

This is how I got sober for good…

I slept

As already mentioned, the first few weeks of sobriety can be exhausting, so I allowed myself to rest whenever I needed to. I took naps during the day, and I went to bed ridiculously early. This also stopped me from spending the evenings obsessing about alcohol, because in the first couple of weeks, it's hard to think about anything else. I knew that my body was healing and I needed to slow down. I'm very lucky I was able to do this, because my boys were able to put themselves to bed and could entertain themselves while I slept after the school run. It would have been a whole different ball game if I was dealing with a baby or toddlers. If you are in the latter bracket, or work long hours, I highly recommend doing anything you can to reduce your daily chores in order to rest. Are you able to take some time off work? If not, can you ask friends and family for some short-term help? If you can afford it, I'd highly recommend getting a cleaner for a few weeks. I was lucky enough to have one when I quit, because I'd not long been separated. Shortly after I became sober, I had to let her go as it became too expensive on my single salary. She was harder to give up than my husband!

When I was drinking, I still went for a five-kilometre run several days a week. I didn't want to stop. I knew that exercise had a really positive effect on my mental health, and I was worried that I would feel worse if I didn't run. But my body was crying out for me to rest. I told myself that I would get back to exercise when my energy levels increased. I knew this would happen after about a month. I just had to follow the timeline (see What Happens When You Stop Drinking – the Timeline).

If you use your narcoleptic period to rest, read, listen to podcasts, watch films that explore the complexities of addiction, and interact with online sober social groups, you can basically kibosh the first 10 per cent of quitting without any effort, and this also really helps with cravings. When you're constantly reading about the effects of alcohol and benefits of sobriety, it keeps your brain focused while you're getting through the early withdrawal stage. I also tried the various suggestions I'd read about in online communities. Painting by numbers is a good example. I thought this was a load of shit, but it was actually pretty therapeutic, and it was a good distraction.

I stuck to basics

As a single mother, I didn't have a live-in partner to rely on to pick up the slack while I was resting. Therefore, I made a conscious decision to focus on the absolute basics and do everything I could to make my life easier. The little energy I had was spent on keeping up with essential chores, feeding my children and working. When I was too tired to cook, I ordered takeout. I shopped online, and I did the bare minimum to keep the house clean and tidy. If something wasn't essential, I gave myself a pass and went easy on myself. Getting sober is a huge life change for the better, and I told myself that everything else could wait. Sobriety was the priority, and I needed to be kind to myself and give myself a break.

As a mum, I was used to running around at a hundred miles an hour, and being lazy was not something I was comfortable with. I think it's easy for mothers to feel guilty when they're not doing what they believe they should be doing. However, I had to let the mum guilt go and recognize that getting sober is the biggest gift I could give to myself and my children. They could cope with a month where we got out of the house less than usual. My boys basically got to spend a huge amount of time watching YouTube and using their tablets. Did they suffer? Nope. They loved it! If they had a choice, they would be on screens constantly anyway! It's a short-term solution that won't hurt them, and in the long run, you'll have the energy to do far more with your kids. Moreover, you'll have the beauty of being present for them for good.

I ate my body weight in sugar

Alcohol contains massive amounts of sugar, and as I've said before, when I first quit, I needed sugar to the extent that I could barely satisfy the craving. I ate cookies until I felt physically sick. Who fucking cares? It's not alcohol. Yes, sugar is bad, but my only concern was staying sober. As long as I didn't drink, I had a tick in the box. To the body, satisfying a craving is all the same, whether it's alcohol or sugar. If your body breathes a sigh of relief when it's getting something that it wants, you feel better. You can sort out your diet later and get back on the treadmill in time. Obviously if you've got any sort of a health condition that is negatively affected by sugar, this is not a wise idea – but in the absence of any other issues, the white stuff is a great tool in early sobriety. Once you're beyond the first month, everything is downhill all the way. Give yourself a break while you're on the uphill climb. As long as you're sober, you're winning.

I organized the shit out of everything

I've read countless books, articles and blogs about getting sober, and so many of them advise focusing on the things you enjoy doing to get through the first few weeks. This only made me feel angry because I had NO dopamine and found NOTHING fun. What was the point in doing things I loved? Firstly, I didn't really have any activities I enjoyed that didn't involve drinking, and secondly, the few things I did enjoy, I didn't want to ruin for myself! What is the point of battling through early sobriety by engaging in enjoyable activities when you have the inability to feel pleasure? It's bloody pointless.

I had a lot of time on my hands. From just after seven when my boys went to bed, I was in thumb-twiddling territory until bedtime. What could I do with this time? I couldn't feel enjoyment, but I could get productive. I could start tackling that to-do list buried in one of those drawers somewhere. I thought to myself that if I could sort out every single cupboard in the house over the next few weeks, by the time my happy hormones came back, I'd then be able to do the stuff I enjoyed – or at least make a start finding out what the hell that was. It seemed like a good plan. It wasn't. It was a fucking amazing one.

When I was drinking, I lived in chaos. My environment was reflective of my mental state. I'd never really read much about the art of feng shui, but it made total sense to me that living in disorder creates a flow of negative energy. I felt it. I always kept a relatively tidy home, but behind the closed doors were levels of carnage that make me cringe just at the memory. I stuffed bills into drawers that were overflowing. I had a wardrobe full of clothes I never wore, and I could never find the things I wanted because so much of it was buried under more clothes. My cupboards were as cluttered as my brain. It made perfect sense to me that organizing my life would create a far more soothing environment to live in.

Once I'd gotten through the narcolepsy stage, I went through my entire home decluttering. I coined a little mantra for myself: "If you can't feel fun, get shit done!" I became obsessed with a show on Netflix called *Get Organized with The Home Edit*. It's basically an entire programme devoted to organizing your house. I fell in love with it. I watched it while I was tidying – and basically copied everything they did. Rainbow-coloured bookshelves in order? Yes, please! A rainbow-ordered wardrobe? Hell, yes! Decanting everything in my kitchen cupboards into plastic boxes with labels? Are you joking? This is like my version of soft porn!

I watched Marie Kondo YouTube videos and learned about only keeping physical things in your home that spark joy – I gave half my wardrobe to charity. I learned how to fold things so you can actually see them and they are not all bunched up in one huge pile. I bought matching wooden coat hangers so everything looked smarter. The end result was a delight to my eyes – and my soul. I know, I know, I sound bat-shit crazy – but don't knock it until you've tried it. Having everything in its place, getting rid of excess crap I didn't need, actually being able to see all of my clothing options, and only keeping the stuff I really liked made a huge difference to how I felt.

By the time I finished, I started to feel happy again – my home looked like something out of a show-home catalogue, but more importantly, it felt completely soothing to walk through my front door. It was peaceful, calm and had a significant impact on my mental state.

Having my home physically organized also yielded some unexpected benefits. I saved loads of time by not having to hunt for things buried in cupboards. Getting the kids ready for school in the morning became a much smoother routine as everything had its place and was easily accessible. Putting laundry away became less of a chore. It's a nice feeling to open the wardrobe and return clothes to their rightful place. My stress levels reduced and I found that I started to sleep even better – because it was comforting to know that everything was in order.

The second thing I set about organizing was my finances. I've always been pretty good with money, but I went through my spreadsheet with a fine-tooth comb and looked at where I could cut back on spending. This was also pivotal in stopping my newfound shopping addiction. When I stopped drinking, I suddenly had a chunk of change in my bank account that would ordinarily have been spent on wine. I guestimated that I'd spent around £4,000 a year on alcohol at home and drinking in bars – a total spend of £100,000 over my drinking career. An insane amount of money. I highly recommend that you calculate how much you've spent on alcohol – and conversely, how much you could save. I will never again use my money to harm myself. This is a lovely thought.

I decided to spend some of the money I was saving on simply enjoying myself, but it also gave me an opportunity to look at where I was overspending in other areas. I cancelled subscriptions I wasn't using, and I changed my bill providers to bring my household running costs down. It quickly became obvious that alcohol was just one of many bad habits I had adopted over the years. I hadn't paid attention to most areas of my life, and they all needed consideration. Quitting alcohol was just the start. Sobriety allowed me to focus on all the other areas, one at a time.

I focused on my time management

Lastly, and most significantly, I adopted a new system of time management. This is one of the most effective and significant changes I made during early sobriety. It has completely transformed the way I use my time and has been the single biggest contributor to reducing my levels of anxiety, second only to giving up alcohol. Motherhood is the mother of all time-suckers. Then we add running a house, having a career, trying to have a social life and exercising – but there are only 24 hours in a day, and I'm pretty sure I'm supposed to spend at least eight of those getting some sleep. However, I couldn't sleep because when I shut my eyes, I would have an endless to-do list bouncing around my head – the "mum list". I must remember to take out the bins, defrost the chicken, pay the school trip fee, buy "X" a birthday gift, make the packed lunches, make a dental appointment, clean the car, pick up the dry-cleaning... Argh!

When I became a single mother, my to-do list increased significantly. When I became sober, I decided that I needed to do something about it. There had to be a better way to effectively manage my time. I felt like I was on a high-speed treadmill, 24/7. I just wanted the world to stop so I could get off for a while.

I'd been a fan of a "list" for as long as I could remember. As a child, I'd watched my mum writing lists for absolutely everything. Her kitchen worksurface looked like a scene from *A Beautiful Mind* – endless lists for endless tasks. The problem with just writing stuff down is that it doesn't have any correlation to the time that we actually have. "Mum lists" basically just look bloody overwhelming. It can be difficult to get the motivation to start something when reaching the end seems totally and utterly impossible.

I decided to abolish my never-ending paper trail, so I wrote one final list containing absolutely everything my brain could think of, and I mean everything. Car insurance needs renewing in nine months' time? On the list. Passport needs renewing in five years' time? On the list. Notes to buy people's gifts a week before their birthdays, school activities – you name it, I wrote it down. Once I'd emptied my head of everything I could think of, I downloaded a Google calendar. Before transferring everything on my list into the calendar, I blocked out time for the most important activity of all: time for myself. I now protect this time like it's a newborn baby. The time for me is non-negotiable. It's not for work, my children or any future partner – it's just for me. This space is in my calendar for at least an hour, every single evening, so I can do whatever I want.

Then I went through each and every item on my list and gave it a time slot in the calendar. Within two hours, my paper list was in the bin, and everything I needed to do was ready to view at the click of a button. I made sure I didn't have more than one significant task per day and that I didn't overload myself. I made

SOBER MAMA

sure there was time for daily house chores. Once I was finished, I felt a huge sense of relief. It felt like I'd completed the list just by transferring it to the calendar. I finally had a system where I wouldn't forget anything, and I didn't need to worry about how I would find the time to get everything done. The time was allocated, and all I needed to do was stick to it.

Of course, there are always days when life gets in the way, or there is some sort of emergency, and things simply can't get done. In this event, I just move the task to a new time slot. It can't be forgotten about – it just gets rescheduled. The single biggest benefit of managing my time in this way is my ability to get to sleep. I never have a to-do list flying around my head when I'm trying to drift off. When I think about all the stuff that needs doing, I just tell myself, "Don't worry – it's on the calendar." If something new pops into my head, I keep a pen and paper next to my bed. I jot down the task and add it to my calendar in the morning.

In a world where technology dominates our human experience, this is one way where it can actually work for you. My schedule remains pretty hectic for the most part, but now I don't worry about finding time. If my calendar starts looking too busy, it's a clear indication to me that something has to give – and I look to see what can be moved or cut out completely. And I will never give up the time for myself. It's too important. However busy my day, I know there is an hour where I can decompress and relax. I know there are days coming where I've allocated the whole day just to have fun. Days where I can be entirely spontaneous with zero guilt – because every task has its place, and I'm free to do what the hell I like with the rest of my time.

Effective time management removes a shit-tonne of stress, helps you sleep, stops feelings of overwhelm, and allows you to have guilt-free time for yourself. Of all the things I've tried to better manage my stress levels in sobriety, this one is right at the top of my list as the most useful.

So good was this exercise that I now teach it to my clients as part of a whole module that deals with organizing your house, finances and general time management. I've become an organization warrior! I highly recommend using your "boredom time" to get things done. When you reach happy hormone town, you'll be in a far better position to really enjoy it, and your life will feel so much more streamlined and peaceful when you're organized.

I got fit and ate like a rabbit

Exercise

We all know that exercising and eating well have endless benefits for both our physical and mental health. However, what I've discovered is that many people struggle to get sober because they want to "fix" everything in one go, and I've seen far too many mums try to get sober, eat like a rabbit and run five kilometres a day, all in the first few weeks. It doesn't work. Why? Because the first couple of months are knackering. It's too much to tackle in one go. Patience is absolutely key. I had no energy at all when

I stopped drinking. I needed to rest. Once I'd got my strength back and organized the shit out of my life, then I was in a far better position to start looking at my physical health.

I ran regularly before I quit drinking, so my first step back to exercise was to start pounding the concrete again. Firstly, it's free and secondly it doesn't demand lots of my time because I don't need to drive to and from a gym. Running is great for overall fitness, with the added benefit of getting you outside. I once saw a quote that said something along the lines of "You can't feel angry or sorry for yourself when you're running." For me, this statement is so true. Whatever negative emotions I'm feeling before a run, I always feel better afterwards. It's a little like a form of meditation, because I can't think negatively while I'm doing it. If I'm mentally working through some issues, a run almost always helps me to find the answers.

Many years ago, I trained to be a yoga instructor, not because I wanted to teach it, but because I fell in love with the practice so much that I wanted to learn more about it. No matter how much I neglect my mat, I always go back to it. It's the perfect workout to try when you're slowly getting back to exercise because it's not tough on your joints, and you don't even need to leave the house. I was recently delighted when I discovered that Netflix now has free yoga classes online. There are also countless options on YouTube. Yoga has been practised for thousands of years and is known to offer many benefits for both the mind and body. Regular practice of yoga can improve flexibility and range of motion, reduce stress and anxiety, build muscle strength, boost the immune system, improve mental clarity and focus, enhance sleep quality and reduce pain and inflammation in the body. Yoga can have an incredible impact on overall health and well-being. It's an ideal form of exercise in early recovery as it helps to calm the mind while you're getting used to feeling your emotions and not having the means to instantly shut them off. If you're a full-time mama and struggle for time alone, you can also get your kids involved too! It's a great way to calm them down and, if you can get your kidlets to follow along with the breathing exercises, it's a fantastic way to get them to shut the fuck up too!

Exercising, after a period of withdrawal and boredom, was like opening bifold doors on a beautiful, sunny day. It lightened my mood and reduced my stress instantaneously. The stronger I became physically, the stronger I became mentally.

Nutrition

Before I gave birth to my eldest son, I never really believed that a healthy diet could make that much of a difference. I had always been skinny, and since weight gain wasn't much of an issue for me, I didn't see any value in eating well. As I mentioned previously, after a disastrous birth, emergency caesarean and a laparotomy, I developed ulcerative colitis – an autoimmune disease with some pretty nasty symptoms. My initial flare-up was so severe that I spent the first six months of my son's life in continual agony.

My uncle put me in touch with a naturopath who supposedly worked miracles with other people who had the same condition as I did. I was sceptical but desperate and willing to try anything. Over a period of a few weeks, my diet was transformed, and I started taking various supplements. The results were staggering. I learned that the human body produces enzymes when we ingest fruits and vegetables. When we eat anything else, the body produces acid to break it down. The source of many diseases starts with the production of acid. When someone is diagnosed with cancer, a plant-based diet is often recommended because cancer thrives in an acidic environment. I had no idea that food could have such an incredible effect on the body's ability to heal.

Once my sugar cravings subsided, I immediately returned to my "colitis diet", which consisted primarily of whole, unprocessed foods (with the exception of coffee – which I LOVE!). While some may view this as an extreme approach, I urge you to give it a chance before dismissing it. Although I was initially worried about missing sugary and unhealthy foods, I quickly lost my desire for them as I began to feel amazing. The benefits were incredible – I had boundless energy, my colitis symptoms decreased, my skin was the clearest it had ever been and I looked radiant. For me, sticking to a clean diet was easy because the alternative caused me constant pain. If you've never tried a clean diet before, you only need to give it a go for a couple of weeks to start feeling the benefits. You'll notice significant changes for the better.

If you're not ready to commit to a completely clean diet, even small positive changes can have a significant impact. Whether it's cutting back on sugar, reducing your intake of processed foods and carbs, or making other healthy substitutions, your body will thank you. Any change for the better is a step in the right direction and, quite often, even small improvements result in massive gains.

I went to therapy

If all you do is stop drinking, you won't address the underlying reasons for why you started drinking in the first place. You won't learn how to effectively cope with life's challenges or manage stress. It's crucial to learn how to navigate life without relying on a crutch. When you remove the one thing you use to deal with all of life's problems, you must confront those problems head-on. If you don't tackle your issues, you may be sober, but you can still feel utterly miserable and anxious. That's exactly where I found myself initially – sober, but feeling like I was climbing the walls. I didn't know how to be an adult, so I reacted to life like a child. I felt scared.

One of the first things I did was to take my sober bum off to therapy. I didn't use an addiction therapist because I knew that alcohol was the secondary problem. The primary issue for me was that I'd never learned how to love myself or cope with adult life, let alone motherhood, without the use of a numbing agent. Therapy is so personal that it is never going to be a one-size-fits-all solution. Some people rave about hypnotherapy. I've tried it, but it did nothing for me. I've tried counselling, and that felt like I was just ranting at someone for an hour a week. It was nice to be able to vent to someone whose sole job is to listen, but I didn't find it massively helpful. I've tried CBT a few times and found it far more successful and enjoyable because it's a pragmatic process that requires taking control of thoughts and actions. I felt much more in control. Some people prefer spiritual therapy. I've not tried it, but for some, it can be a huge source of comfort and resonate more than traditional therapy.

For me, the key is quite simply having someone independent to talk to who can help you work through your thoughts and worries, and who isn't a close friend or family member. Therapists of any kind are objective and have one goal – to help you. They're not clouded by feelings or connection with you. Friends and family have the best intentions, but that doesn't mean you're getting good advice. Wherever there is skin in the game, there is a distinct lack of objectivity, and it's so much easier to be totally honest with a stranger.

Just try whatever feels right for you. You've got nothing to lose by giving it a go. Alcohol costs a fortune. People pay for it because they see value in drinking. When you see more value in the benefits of sobriety, it's an easy trade to spend your booze money on investing in yourself. There is no point in spending money on the things you love if you're not in a headspace to actually enjoy them. I've previously spent thousands on holidays from which I've got no pleasure, because I was in such a bad place mentally. By investing in my mental health first, it's meant that every penny I've spent since can actually be enjoyed.

I was accountable

The biggest piece of advice I can give, more than anything else I've written, is to not go through the process of quitting alone. Find a programme where you are accountable to someone. For me, accountability is the cornerstone of quitting alcohol. Of all the feedback I've received from my mum clients, accountability is the top reason why my method worked for them. There are countless programmes out there. While I believe AA has its flaws, I do think that their methodology of having a sponsor is likely to be the main reason for the success of those participants. I tried to quit so many times, and one of the main reasons I repeatedly failed is that I kept the struggle to myself. I suffered alone.

Connecting with others who are trying to get sober or have already made the transition is truly the best medicine.

I set goals

What does a happy life look like to you? If you could wave a magic wand, where would you be one year from now, and what would your life look like? What would you be doing? My therapist once asked me these same questions, and I couldn't answer. I told her that I had no idea what a happy life looked like for me. I couldn't envision what I needed, or even wanted for myself. She then asked me, "How do you know what you need to do with your life now and what actions you need to take if you don't know where you want to be?"

My therapist set me a challenge to write down three long-term goals and three short-term ones. It took me a few days to really think about this. Once I decided, it became evident why she had set this exercise for me. I couldn't achieve any of my long-term goals without first tackling the short-term ones. The short-term goals were simply the actions I needed to take to get where I wanted to be in the future.

I was given the task to read my goal list before I went to sleep every night and then again when I woke up each morning. I was to do this every day until a goal was met, and then I had to cross it off the list. Once completed, I would make a new list. My therapist explained that every single day, if our actions aren't aligned with our goals and what we want from life, we're not going to achieve happiness. By writing our goals down, we have a road map, and we know what actions we need to take in the here and now.

This simple exercise was an incredible turning point for me. By writing down my goals, I started to realize that the only way I was going to get the life I really wanted was by tackling the short-term action list. I continue to use this exercise to this day, as it keeps me focused and driven to achieve the life that I want for myself. One of my long-term goals was to write this book. My short-term goal was to commit to writing 1,000 words a day. By reading this goal every night and every morning, I motivated myself to take action. My long-term goal of getting a book published would never happen if I didn't commit to writing each day. It sounds simple, but up until that point, writing a book was something I thought about regularly, but never actually started.

When I was drinking, all of my dreams for the future were just that – dreams. I was forever procrastinating and never taking action. When you're newly sober, you have so much time! What can you do with yours? Just work out what you want, write your goals down and start taking action.

Will I Ever Laugh Again?

"The most wasted day of all is that in which we have not laughed."

Nicolas Chamfort

"Will I ever laugh again?" This is a question I asked myself over and over in the first couple of months of sobriety. I kept thinking of that scene in the first *Sex and the City* movie, where Carrie Bradshaw is in Mexico with her girlfriends. She was supposed to be on holiday with her new husband, but the groom never made it to the altar. Carrie is heartbroken and asks her friends if she will ever laugh again. Her friend Miranda reassures her that she will, when something is really, really funny.

I've thought about this scene often. Okay, I hadn't been jilted at the altar by a man, but I had been through a break-up of sorts when I stopped drinking. I had been in a relationship with alcohol for 25 years. But even toxic relationship break-ups are hard to recover from. It takes time.

Carrie does laugh again in the movie. When her friend Charlotte shits herself. I wondered if I would have a defining moment when I would laugh like that – so hard that my stomach hurt. Whether a time would come when my life could be enjoyable sober. When I wouldn't believe that I needed alcohol to relax and have fun. I didn't honestly believe that I would ever experience that soul-lifting kind of laughter again.

When I think back to the times where I drank and laughed – it wasn't so much because of the alcohol I consumed. It was watching the effect of alcohol on other people. Watching them behave in a way that was amusing to me – because their inhibitions were lowered. They behaved so differently to how they did when they were sober. Now when I see people doing crazy things when they've been drinking, I simply don't find it funny. I'm not on the same wavelength. Do I miss this? Yes, at times. But for every drunken story I've got with a funny anecdote, I've got twice as many that end badly. Alcohol causes chaos. You never know what lowered inhibitions are going to result in. Something amusing or something disastrous. It's like tossing a coin. Pot luck.

I loved the idea of being sober and not making a fool of myself anymore. Of not saying and doing things that are incongruent with my values. Of being stable. Reliable. But I didn't want to lose the laughter. What if that never came back? What if I never found anything as funny again? Was I set for a life of monotony in order to feel safe and be healthy? I wanted a luminescent life. Sobriety looked so, well, beige to me.

During a particularly difficult week in my first sober year, I decided to book a spa weekend in Hampshire, with my dear friend Kelly. I spent the first day trying to relax, read my book and tried to stop my brain from spinning like a waltzer on turbo speed. But I couldn't chill out. I felt so wired, tightly wound and downright miserable. I repeatedly apologized to Kelly for being such bloody awful company.

"No! You're not! You're just having a bit of a shit time. It will get better. Let's go in the hot tub. That will help to relax your body."

I reluctantly agreed. I didn't even want to get wet. That would mean I needed to get dry again. Too much fucking energy. As I sat in the hot tub, I felt a little soothed by the bubble jets on my back and my body began to ever so slightly succumb to the water pressure. There were about eight other people in there with us. Everyone avoiding eye contact and trying to keep themselves to themselves. So British! I definitely would have felt more comfortable if it was just the two of us. I'm evidently very British too.

"Do you know what? Since I've had the girls, my vagina is fucked," Kelly said. She was not quiet.

I grinned a little. Kelly has zero filter. She has a mouth like a trucker, says whatever pops into her head, and then spits it out with no shame. I love her for this. It's especially funny because she doesn't care who is within earshot. The eight people in the hot tub could hear every word. Kelly didn't bat an eyelid.

She continued, "Do you want to know how bad it is? Imagine going to a kebab van. Close your eyes. No, I mean it. Close your eyes now." I duly obliged and closed my eyes.

"Right. Good. Now really concentrate. Visualize a kebab van. Walk over to the van and order a large doner kebab in a huge pitta bread. Now you need to ask for some chilli sauce and mayo. Squeeze a load of that on there. Now mush it all up together. Oh shit. You just dropped it on the floor! It's gone fucking everywhere. Pick it up. Ten-second rule. Scrape the doner meat off the pavement back into the pitta. You've missed the sauce. Scrape that back in too. Now look at the kebab. Look at the fucking state of it. That's my fanny. That's exactly what my fanny looks like since I've had my girls. Loose as fuck and shit hanging out everywhere. Fucking motherhood."

I instantly started to howl with laughter. I had tears rolling down my face.

Kelly continued, "I don't even care anymore... The other day Maisie and Lottie [her daughters] came into the bathroom when I was getting ready for a shower. Maisie looked at my bits and asked, 'Why is it so hairy?'

'Because I'm single!' I told her.

Maisie said, 'But it's so big. Can we call it Hagrid?'

Lottie threw her hands in the air shouting, 'Oh no! It's a Gruffalo!'"

I screeched out loud and clutched my stomach in pain. Beautiful pain caused by excruciatingly gorgeous laughter. I looked up after a few seconds and saw the eight people in the hot tub, all trying to avoid my gaze. The shoulders gave them all away. Bobbing up and down in unison. Desperately trying to hide the fact they'd been eavesdropping and failing to hide their stifled giggles. I laughed and laughed and laughed. For about ten solid minutes. For the rest of the day, Kelly and

I would spontaneously erupt into fits of giggles, just at the memory of the hot tub and the reactions of those eight other people. That one story was an instant antidote to my feelings of anxiety on that day. It lifted my soul.

Kelly purposefully told that story at that time, knowing how to make me laugh and recognizing that I needed to. She is truly a tonic, and I feel eternally grateful and blessed to call her my friend. That moment in the hot tub will forever serve as a reminder to me that life is good and laughter truly is the best medicine. Sobriety doesn't remove fun, but rather it allows you to experience it fully and remember it without dulled senses. It's truly beautiful.

If you find yourself struggling with the belief that you can't have fun without alcohol, the best way to challenge this belief is to search for evidence to the contrary. Take a moment to scroll back through your memories and remember a time when you had fun without alcohol, perhaps laughing so hard that you cried.

Before the hot tub incident, I looked for instances where I had genuinely enjoyed life without being under the influence. The only prolonged period of sobriety I had experienced was during my pregnancies, and it was during this time that I had a cherished memory that proved it was possible to find happiness and laughter, without relying on alcohol. I vividly remember sitting on my bed, heavily pregnant and preparing to sleep while my then husband was in the adjacent en suite. Abruptly, I heard him shout, "Argh!" as he stormed out of the bathroom, visibly frustrated and annoyed.

"Why can't you put the lids back on stuff properly? All I did was put my hand in the drawer, and now I'm bloody covered in your body butter," he complained.

It was true. I rarely put the lid back on my body butter properly. It seemed pointless to do so when I was using it so regularly. I was determined to come out of pregnancy without stretch marks, so I regularly doused myself with copious amounts of body butter and Bio-Oil.

"It's hardly the end of the world. Just wash it off," I replied, trying not to smile.

"I can't! It's too thick and greasy!"

"Well just rub it in then! It can't hurt you. You might even like it! It will make your skin soft."

I have a vivid memory of my ex-husband reluctantly rubbing the cream over his face with a grimace. It wouldn't rub in. It just stayed on the surface and looked more like a face mask. I started to smirk. Then I looked closer.

"Come here a second," I said curiously.

He walked closer.

"That's not my body butter. My body butter is pink. It's cherry flavour."

I suddenly realized what the cream was.

"Er, sorry to tell you, but you've just covered your face with my Anusol."

"Argh! Are you fucking joking! No way!"

My ex-husband ran back to the bathroom and hastily began scraping my haemorrhoid cream off his face, all the while cussing. I burst into raucous laughter, finding it increasingly amusing the angrier he became. Out of all the creams in that drawer, it had to be the tube that split. So, ladies, take note: if your husband is behaving like an arsehole, there's a cream for that.

Look for evidence that happiness and fun aren't solely dependent on alcohol. If you really think about it, you'll find countless memories of joyful moments that have nothing to do with drinking. Will you ever laugh again if you become sober? Yes, of course you will – when something is really funny.

Relapse – and Being Careful Who You Accept Advice From

> "It's not about how many times you fall; it's about how many times you get back up."

Anonymous

The dreaded "R" word. No one wants to be there, but unfortunately, it can happen easily if you still believe that there is some value to drinking – and more often than not, this belief is subconscious. If you do pick up a glass again, there is a little voice in your brain telling you that something good will come from it – even if you are actively trying to convince yourself otherwise. Unravelling beliefs about alcohol takes time, a lot of "quit lit", introspective learning and much self-reflection. It is really common to relapse while you are still learning how to get and stay sober, so try not to beat yourself up. As long as you keep trying, you are on the right path. In the meantime, if you do relapse, try this trick to prevent further occurrences…

Commit to taking a two-minute video of yourself for every glass you pour. Answer three questions to the camera:

1. *How do you feel right now mentally?*
2. *What physical sensations do you feel?*
3. *Rate your level of anxiety from one to ten. Rate your level of depression from one to ten.*

Then record one more video when you first wake up. Ask yourself the same questions.

I can assure you that there is no better deterrent for craving alcohol than watching playback of all your videos, especially the last one of the night. There is nothing more unappealing than seeing yourself as a drunken, slurring mess. It may not be the most comfortable viewing, but it is undoubtedly effective. When we drink, we often look and sound far worse than we perceive ourselves to be.

You will notice that with every glass, your anxiety will initially decrease. The following morning, both your anxiety and depression scores will be higher than the previous night, before you started drinking. The trade-off for momentarily reducing your anxiety is that it will come back worse the next day, and with an added dose of depression.

So, if you do relapse, try this trick. You have nothing to lose, and you will be amazed at how you appear and sound after several drinks – it's never what we expect. After seeing the footage, you will not want to look or sound like that again, and it will become a powerful preventive tool alongside the other tricks and tips you decide to use.

Building your own toolbox of strategies and coping mechanisms is crucial when it comes to navigating the challenging road to sobriety. It's also important to seek support and advice from others; however, it's crucial to be discerning about who we take advice from. Not everyone has the knowledge or experience to provide effective guidance on matters related to sobriety. Well-meaning friends or family members who still drink alcohol may not fully understand the complexities of addiction and the process of recovery. For a non-addict, it can be very difficult to comprehend.

During my early days of recovery, I encountered well-meaning individuals who would say things like "Just have one drink, it won't hurt" or "You're not an alcoholic; you just need to learn how to control yourself." While they may have had good intentions, their advice was as useful as me asking a fox for guidance on how to protect a henhouse.

Comments like these reminded me of the time when I was using Supernanny's (TV personality Jo Frost) advice on bedtime routines. I'd been using her technique for weeks and I was failing miserably. My son Alfie was just 18 months old and every time I put him to bed, he would crawl back downstairs. I tried Supernanny's method of walking him back to bed, saying "bedtime" and leaving the room, but after 62 times of doing this, I was ready to pull my hair out. I had a glass of red wine in hand as I pondered what to do next. I googled the technique, to make sure I was doing it properly. I discovered that Supernanny doesn't have any children. Why the fuck was I taking advice from this woman?!

In a tipsy state, I decided to come up with my own technique. There had to be a better way than marching my son back to bed 62 times. The next time I put Alfie back to bed, I hid in the corner of his bedroom in the dark. When he climbed out of bed, I used the scariest monster voice I could muster and screeched, "GET BACK TO BED!" Alfie screamed, ran, jumped into his bed and pulled the covers over his head. I immediately switched back to "mummy" mode and reassured him that the monster was gone – as long as he went to sleep.

Did I scar my son for life? Maybe. Did I get the "mum of the year" award? Definitely not. But did it work? Absolutely! From that night on, Alfie never got up again. Supernanny's technique may be good in theory, but she doesn't have any skin in the game. Her technique just didn't work for me as a tired, emotionally drained and worn-out mum who had already climbed the stairs 62 times in one night and had to be up for work in the morning.

Every child is different, and what works for one may not work for another. It's the same for getting sober – it's crucial to be discerning about who you turn to for guidance. Look for those who have personally experienced the journey and emerged on the other side with newfound strength and vitality. The people who have succeeded.

I read Matthew Perry's memoir, *Friends, Lovers, and the Big, Terrible Thing*, the week before he passed away. I was a huge fan and I read this book cover to cover in the space of a day. I remember thinking how astounding it was that he was still standing after the levels of abuse he put his body through. How terribly sad that this statement is no longer true. One thing I found really interesting was that Perry recommended AA. I was completely inspired by Perry's story, but I certainly was not inspired to follow suit with the methods that he used. Perry spent several million dollars on recovery but, ultimately, he spent a whole lifetime relapsing.

Reading stories about other addicts is incredibly humbling and fascinating – but what really helps is following in the footsteps of the people who beat addiction swiftly, painlessly and go on to lead a healthy and happy life. The ones who make it look easy. If you follow in the footsteps of the people that struggle for a lifetime, what are the chances you'll do the same?

Ultimately, no one knows your journey better than you do. And if anyone tries to tell you otherwise, just smile and nod – and then go find someone who actually knows what they're talking about. Look to those who have smashed addiction in the face and are now living their best life. You wouldn't take business advice from someone who never ran a business or had become bankrupt and failed professionally. You want advice from the billionaire who is raking it in. It's no different when seeking advice about sobriety. Follow success and you are far more likely to succeed too.

Socializing Sober

> "The most basic and powerful way to connect to another person is to listen. Just listen. Perhaps the most important thing we ever give each other is our attention."

Rachel Naomi Remen

The fear of a sober social life was one of the many worries that kept me stuck in active addiction. I couldn't possibly enjoy time out with friends without my best friend, Pinot Grigio, being present. The thought alone made me wince. In my first few weeks of sobriety, I didn't want to go out. I didn't want to see people. I certainly didn't think I would enjoy myself.

When I first started to venture out, I decided to stick to daytime activities only. I didn't feel safe going to a bar because I knew it would be too triggering for me. I didn't keep alcohol in the house and to this day, I still don't. If friends come over for dinner, I politely ask them to bring themselves and whatever they're drinking. I no longer crave alcohol at all, and I don't believe I would ever slip. However, keeping alcohol in a cupboard is like letting your kids have a sleepover with ten kids.

It's survivable, but why would you want to when you can just avoid it?

I started going out by keeping it short and sweet. Heading out for coffee was okay because I did that anyway. It didn't feel unusual, and there was no risk I would drink wine. I got to see friends and have a chat – painless and actually quite enjoyable. The more I went out, the more I desired to do it again. I quickly realized that socializing is just a glorified term for something far simpler – talking! That's all socializing actually is. We spend time with people, talk to them and listen. Any activity we do in tandem is actually pretty superfluous. Think about it – when you go to a bar, other than consuming alcohol, all you are actually doing is spending time with your friends, speaking to them and enjoying their company. It's the same sober, only with way more perks.

I have spent many drunken nights with friends that I don't really remember much about, least of all the conversation. Now, when I spend time with people, I remember everything. They have my undivided attention, and I actually listen. I used to think that getting blasted, wearing my heart on my sleeve, confessing all my secrets, crying, hugging in the bathroom and divulging my deep love for those closest to me, was a form of connection. Sometimes even with total strangers! In actuality, it was merely the result of lowered inhibitions. True connection is only possible when I'm mentally present – when it's me who's actually talking, not the lubricated version that blurts out the first thing that pops into her brain.

It's easy to see how this type of "connection" is a myth once you're sober. I'm sure that at some point, you have been in the company of a friend who is wasted when you're not drinking yourself. When they slur, cry and tell you that you mean everything to them, do you feel connected? Or do you simply put their ultra-display of affection down to too much alcohol? Do you feel like you're bonding, or do you simply hope they won't have a crushing hangover the next day and help them to bed?

I have found that since I've been sober, my friends are also far more likely to confide in me and ask for advice. There has been a significant shift in how I show up for other people, and they feel it. It's not that I didn't care about my friends before; I was just living in total and utter bedlam. Now, I am much more thoughtful. If a friend tells me she has a job interview, I make a note to send her a message to wish her luck. In my drinking days, I would easily forget little things like this. They're fairly inconsequential when you forget, but they mean a great deal to others when you remember. I'm just a whole lot more consistent and reliable than I used to be.

I felt fairly confident going out to meet friends when I got sober, but what about heading out to social events that involve people you don't know very well – this can be pretty daunting. The term "Dutch courage" is used to describe false confidence derived from consuming alcohol, and many people use booze for this purpose, to navigate social situations they aren't particularly comfortable with. So how do you do this when you're newly sober, feeling vulnerable and navigating unchartered waters? By recognizing that you are perfectly capable and you do this ALL the time, on a daily basis, without the use of alcohol. We have countless interactions with people we don't know that well or don't know at all. In the supermarket, the office, any high street store, asking for directions in the street, at the doctor's office, at the school gates... you get my point. The list is endless. You don't need the lubrication of alcohol for any of these things, yet talking to people in a bar with a soft drink in hand seems utterly terrifying! The truth is that we don't need alcohol to talk to people. We just don't like those first few minutes of awkwardness and small talk. Once you're five minutes into a conversation, the awkwardness ebbs away. Once you've been out and successfully handled a couple of nights sober, you will naturally grow in confidence.

If you want to give yourself an added confidence boost, stick on some empowering music before you go out and dance around the kitchen – this can have a significant positive effect on your mood and mentality. Buy yourself a killer dress and some new make-up with the money you're saving by not drinking. Even two weeks sober your skin will be glowing, and you'll be surprised at how many people notice how good you look. The changes in appearance over the first month are honestly staggering. Glam up and strut your stuff! It won't be long before you're loving your new sober nights out.

Another worry you may experience if you're going out to bars is whether you will be hit by a craving. It's different for everyone, but I am a firm believer that if you have any doubts, it's just so much easier to avoid the situation until you're ready.

Job done. The difficulties arise when you have occasions to go to that you can't avoid, such as a friend's wedding. I quit drinking right before the Christmas party season, and I managed to avoid most events, but for the few I couldn't get out of, I made myself a plan in advance. There is nothing worse than being stuck at a party you can't leave and then getting a craving. I always made sure I had an exit strategy.

Firstly, I would always have an excuse for why I wasn't drinking – I was driving. I told people I couldn't even have one, as I don't feel safe driving with any alcohol in my system. It stopped the questions. I didn't want to have conversations about my decision not to drink. It took every ounce of my brainpower to stay sober. I simply didn't have the energy to talk or, worse, argue about it with other people. I wanted to talk about it when I was ready. And for me, ready meant "no longer craving". Wanting alcohol and not being able to have it made me feel extremely vulnerable – far easier to avoid triggering conversations entirely.

Secondly, I would lie. Yep. I told big fat porky pies. Why? Because they were white lies, didn't hurt anyone and I still got to go out while simultaneously protecting my sobriety, like it was a newborn baby. I also always had something that I needed to be up early for the next day. This meant I could justify leaving early, without getting into the conversation about why I was going. I'd sometimes start an evening with some sort of fictitious ailment, usually the onset of a migraine. When I arrived at an evening function, I would announce that I had the onset of a migraine and ask around to see if anyone had any paracetamol. If I enjoyed the evening and felt comfortable, the paracetamol would miraculously cure my headache, and I'd stay and have a good time. If I felt triggered and wanted to get the fuck out of there, I simply told people that my migraine had become much worse and I needed to leave. Cue lots of "Ahs" and "Oh, you poor thing" comments, and people wouldn't give me any grief about going. I could just slip out the door with no bother. In fact, I've noticed that if I stay long enough at any event involving alcohol, no one actually cares when I leave. They don't notice. After around the fourth drink, people aren't even going to remember their own night, let alone whether I left at nine or midnight.

As it turns out, I find going out isn't only easy to do while sober – it's better! Firstly, I now have far more options. I can plan things on a school night and drive. With no hangover to worry about, the world is my oyster. I can also go further afield. Recently, I decided impromptu to drive to a stand-up comedy venue. It was 40 minutes away, and if I was drinking, I would have needed to go by rail and change trains twice. Plus, it was very cold, so being able to go door-to-door in the comfort of a warm car was brilliant. Pretty much everyone at the venue was drinking. A couple of men were so drunk that they started heckling and got kicked out of the club. By the end of the evening, so many people looked worse for wear, and it was delightful to drive home knowing that I would wake up feeling great – and I actually remembered the evening. The biggest downside to going to alcohol-heavy venues is that you lose touch with people around the third or fourth drink. I can have meaningful conversations with them up until this point, and then after that, we're just on totally different wavelengths. By the time other people are intoxicated, slurring their words and repeating themselves, I duck out. I enjoy the time I'm out and feel no shame in leaving early.

I've become a huge fan of an early night. After a few hours of socializing, I'm more than ready for some time alone and some peace and quiet. I thought sobriety would make me tedious company, but it turns out it's actually just made drunk people really boring to be around. I just know when to leave the party – and I can walk out the door rather than falling through it.

Sober socializing can take a little getting used to, but I promise it's nothing to be feared and it quickly becomes your "new normal", as much as I loathe the term. You can go where you want, when you want and leave as soon as you need to. The sense of freedom is exhilarating, and there are so many doors opened when you don't require constant access to a bar.

Sober Holidays

"A trip is what you take when you can't take
any more of what you've been taking."

Adeline Ainsworth

Going on a holiday is an exciting and often much-needed break from the stresses of daily life – especially for mums – although one could easily argue that if you've got your kids with you, it's not really a holiday! When I was drinking, holidays were just a great excuse to drink all day long and do very little else, starting from the arrival at the airport, even if it was first thing in the morning. It would be rude not to, obviously. The last drinking holiday I went on was probably the most boozy trip I've ever taken. It was October 2021 and about a month before I decided to quit for good. That holiday was certainly a catalyst for my decision, as I had my first experience of shaking in the morning and by the time I got home, I felt like I'd been beaten up from the inside out.

I went away with my dad, my friend Kelly, my boys and her two girls. We were flying to Barcelona and boarding a cruise ship for a trip around the Med. It was an early flight so we needed to leave at 5 a.m. Obviously I went to bed early so I'd be well rested and got up bright and early, excited for the trip. Yeah right. My dad and I polished off a couple of bottles of wine the night before – because holidays evidently start the very second you finish work – and I woke up at 5 a.m. feeling hungover and absolutely dog rough. So rough that I missed our turning for the airport on the motorway and added 30 minutes to our journey. Never mind. I'd booked the lounge. All would be right with the world as soon as I got my hands on a glass of champagne. Holidays are there to be celebrated!

We checked our bags in and headed straight for the lounge. My boys got stuck into breakfast and my dad and I got stuck into the bar. We were both in a bad way at that time. My dad was in the midst of an intense period of grieving and really quite broken, while I was in the middle of my divorce and just a total anxious mess. Copious amounts of alcohol was the only solution.

As it turns out, we actually arrived at the airport far too early for our flight, despite my unexpected detour, so we had over two hours to wait in the lounge. Enough time for me to down five glasses of champagne and my dad, five glasses of red wine. By the time we left and went to meet Kelly at the gate, we were already pissed.

We all got onto the plane and took our seats. I went to put the passports in my handbag and suddenly realized I'd only got three of them.

"Dad? Have you got your passport? I've only got three of them."

"No! I gave mine to you! Are you joking?!" Dad sounded totally frantic. He does tend to worry about small things, and to be fair to him, this could potentially have been a bit of a disaster.

"Er, I've lost one. I had it at the gate. I must have done or they wouldn't have let us on the plane."

With that, my dad shot out of his seat, barked at the airhostess in the doorway that he needed to find a passport, and ran down the gangway shouting "PASSPORT, PASSPORT!" at the line of people waiting to board the plane. Thinking that my dad was some sort of crazed official, people started to show my dad *their* passports. At that point I could hear his exasperated yelling – "NO! LOST PASSPORT! LOST PASSPORT!"

Kelly was sat in the seat in front of me. She turned around looking utterly confused.

"What the fuck is going on?" she said.

"I've lost one of the bloody passports."

"What do you mean? You've got four right there."

I looked down and sure enough, there were all four passports. I was just so drunk that I couldn't see straight. Oh shit. A very nice chap next to me offered to go and get my dad back, so he also went running off down the gangway to stop the old man from venturing too far. When they returned, my dad was purple in the face, sweating profusely and hyperventilating. But fuck me, it was funny. My dad, Kelly and I spent the entire flight in fits of giggles. It's only now I look back and see how horribly wrong that could have gone. I could easily have dropped a passport. We could have easily missed our flight.

The plane debacle was just the start of our boozy antics. We continued to drink on the flight, and when we got to Barcelona, we headed straight for the hotel bar. Our drinks arrived and the waitress slipped, spilling an entire glass of red wine down my dad's shirt. By this point we were all plastered, so this seemed like one of the most hysterical things that's ever happened. We laughed so raucously that our group was the focus of everyone in the hotel bar – and not in a good way. We must have been so annoying to everyone trying to quietly enjoy their own holidays. Kelly's daughter filmed the whole incident on her tablet. It was incredibly amusing to watch back the next day, but there is no escaping the fact that we were all completely hammered and looked a right state. There is also no denying that this situation was funny – but you never know whether a drinking session is going to produce some amusing anecdote or something far more sinister. It's like a game of Russian Roulette. For every funny drinking story, I have a cringeworthy or dangerous one. The ones that beat you round the head at 3 a.m. and tell you that you're clearly a terrible person. The risk is simply not worth the reward. Had I actually lost a passport, it would have been horrendous. The whole week on the cruise was spent hopping from bar to bar. The kids had a whale of a time on the waterslides and in kids' club – an added bonus that meant we could get leathered in peace.

This was the first time in my life that I really felt the need to have a morning drink. I woke up one morning, a few days into the cruise, and by 9 a.m. I could feel that I was shaky. I started to have a panic attack on the cruise deck and had to sit down while Kelly talked me through a slow breathing exercise. I knew damn well it was withdrawal. That made the panicking worse. My God, if I'm shaking and having a panic attack, I'm really in trouble. Maybe I actually am an alcoholic now! My kidneys hurt. I could feel them pulsating in my back. Only one thing for it. I ordered a mimosa. Totally acceptable morning drink. It's a breakfast accompaniment after all. I resigned myself to the fact that I wasn't going to be able to quit drinking on that cruise, but I promised myself then and there that I would have a period of abstinence when I got home. I once read that it takes six weeks for the liver to heal. I'll just take six weeks off and then I'll be good as new.

After the holiday I did abstain for a few days, but as expected, I quickly ended up going back to old faithful Pinot Grigio. But the intensity of the panic remained and it wasn't more than a few weeks until I hit the point where I was sick and tired of feeling sick and tired. When I quit drinking for good, I was terrified at the prospect of a sober holiday. I believed I would be totally bored and not enjoy myself at all. It couldn't have been further from the truth. Sober, holidays are the absolute best. Recently I took a trip to Budapest. Having been there before, I wasn't interested in the sightseeing again, so I looked for other activities. I wound up spending an exorbitant amount of time navigating various escape rooms. It was the most fun I'd had in years. Alcohol isn't necessary to have a great holiday – in fact, alcohol often ruins most holidays as you wake up hungover daily and feel like you need another holiday to get over the one you've just been on. Sober, you can really make the most of the places you see and the company you keep. It's also completely illuminating to wake up fresh for the day ahead and excited to get out and actually see more than the inside of a bar.

In early recovery from addiction, going away can present unique challenges as you begin to navigate new environments and potentially triggering situations. However, with some careful planning, it is easy to enjoy a fun and fulfilling trip away, without the need for alcohol. Here are my tips for travelling sober.

Choose your destination carefully

When planning a holiday, it's important to consider the potential triggers that may arise in certain locations. For example, if you are in recovery from alcohol addiction, it may be best to avoid destinations that are known for their party culture or heavy drinking scenes. Instead, consider places that offer opportunities for relaxation and rejuvenation, such as a beach holiday or a wellness retreat. Alternatively, you may want to choose a destination that aligns with your interests or hobbies, such as a hiking or cycling trip, where alcohol is not a central part of the experience. I'd also suggest avoiding cruise ships entirely. I took a cruise about nine months into my sober journey. I felt solid in my recovery and I didn't even consider that being in this environment would be triggering, as I was long past the point of craving alcohol. I was surprised at just how difficult I found it to be around so many people who constantly had a cocktail in hand. I had nowhere to escape to. At every turn, there was another bar. I'll absolutely consider cruising in the future, but in early sobriety, I'd advocate a clear miss on this one.

Plan your itinerary

Planning your holiday itinerary in advance is like plotting a sober revolution. You gotta be strategic, people! No impulsive decisions that'll lead you down the slippery slope of temptation. So, skip the boozy activities and opt for adventures that don't involve alcohol. Sightseeing, hiking, bungee jumping (if you're feeling brave), you name it. And when it comes to dining and entertainment, research no-alcohol alternatives like alcohol-free bars and restaurants, museums or other attractions. And whatever you do, don't fall for the all-inclusive trap. That's like willingly walking into a lion's den covered in steak sauce. Just ask the hotel to remove the alcohol from your mini-bar, and you're good to go. Alternatively, you can remove loads of temptation by avoiding hotels altogether and renting a villa. For a start, hotels love to offer welcome drinks and it's not so easy to resist when a cocktail is thrust into your hands and you don't even need to pay for it. Staying away from hotels also gives you the autonomy to design your own holiday privately without having to circumvent the bar. A villa has some other added bonuses – you're not being subjected to the shitty nightly entertainment, other peoples' screaming kids (sorry, you can't do much about your own) and unsavoury guests. With a little bit of planning and a lot of determination, you'll have the sober holiday of your dreams.

Practise self-care

You thought taking care of yourself was important before? Well, on holiday, it's like you're on self-care steroids. You've got to prioritize activities that'll keep you sane, like exercise, meditation and journalling. It's all about balance. Don't forget to get enough sleep, too. Otherwise, you'll end up like a kid on a sugar low, except instead of craving sweets, you'll be eyeing that bottle of tequila like it's your long-lost lover. So, take care of yourself, get some rest and keep those pesky urges at bay. You got this, sober warrior!

Have a plan for cravings

You know what's worse than dealing with a stressful new environment? Dealing with a new stressful environment – without a drink in your hand. It's like trying to juggle flaming swords while riding a unicycle, not an easy task. So, what do you do? You plan, my friend. You bring a list of distractions that can save your sanity when the urge to drink hits. Call a friend, do some deep breathing, start a knitting project – whatever floats your sober boat. And don't forget your support system. You need a crew of people who have your back, like a sponsor or a recovery group. They're like your personal cheerleaders, minus the pom-poms and the short skirts. With these tools in your sobriety toolbox, you can conquer any new environment and emerge victorious, sober and still standing.

Navigating airports and planes

I never realized how hard it is to just walk into an airport when you're sober. I mean, the airport bar used to be my first stop after checking in. That was the moment my holiday started as far as I was concerned. But now, it's like trying to resist a chocolate cake when you're on a diet. It's tough, especially when your flight is delayed. So, I've learned to come prepared. I bring books, games, puzzles, anything to keep my mind off the bar. And when I go through passport control, I stock up on drinks for the flight. It's so much easier to say, "No thanks" to the cart lady when you've got a bottle of water in your hand or just pretend to be asleep to avoid the conversation entirely. And if you're a nervous flyer, like me, you can always visit the doc for some anxiety medication for the flight. Trust me, you don't want to be in a situation where you're stressed out and the only option is to drown your worries in booze. That's just asking for trouble. Stay sober, and enjoy the ride!

Have fun!

Above all else, have fun! Holidays are a time for us to kick back and let go of all the daily drama. You don't need to be fuelled by alcohol to have a good time. No hangovers means you can remember every moment and make some unforgettable memories. Trust me, since I started staying sober on my trips, I've had some of the wildest and craziest adventures ever! And the best part? No more post-holiday detox needed. Back in the day, I'd always come home feeling like I needed to enter rehab. But now, I look forward to every holiday like a kid on Christmas morning, because every moment is a chance for an epic story. What will your next adventure look like?

Finding Fun

"The highest form of research is essentially play."

N. V. Scarfe

The hedonic treadmill is a concept that refers to our tendency to adapt to new positive experiences and return to our baseline level of happiness. In other words, no matter how much we indulge in pleasurable activities, such as drinking alcohol, our happiness will eventually plateau and we'll need more of it to feel the same level of pleasure. This is particularly relevant in alcohol recovery, where the hedonic treadmill can lead to relapse. After giving up alcohol, it can be tempting to seek out other sources of pleasure to fill the void. But, as the hedonic treadmill reminds us, these new sources will eventually lose their lustre and we'll be back at square one – it can be a real buzzkill. It's like chasing after a high that you can never truly reach, like trying to fill a bottomless beer mug. Learning to find fun and happiness in sobriety is about learning to enjoy the moment, instead of the relentless pursuit of happiness in the future: "If I just have x, y, z... then I'll be happy."

When we drink alcohol, it's like trying to run on a treadmill while someone keeps increasing the speed. It's a never-ending battle. The only way to truly win the game is to hop off the treadmill altogether and find joy in the simple things in life, like a good cup of coffee or a warm hug from a loved one. And let's be honest, those things are a lot cheaper than a night at the bar.

Before getting sober, I can't think of many activities that I enjoyed that didn't involve alcohol. Most of my social life revolved around bar-hopping. I lived for social nights out at the pub, day drinking sessions in London, and boozy brunches. As far as I was concerned, whatever I was doing for enjoyment was made better with the presence of wine. Cinema? Yep, I could bring wine in a flask. Day trip to the beach? Absolutely, Prosecco in the picnic basket.

I signed up for some sober Facebook groups and found several posts relating to my struggle to find enjoyable sober activities. I was NOT impressed with some of the suggestions I read:

- *Take up knitting*
- *Try paint-by-numbers*
- *Get some colouring books*

What. The. Actual. Fuck. No way. Was this what my sober life was going to look like now? No getting glammed up for hot nights out on the town? No excitement? Just fucking knitting and painting pictures of peacocks and unicorns that look so shitty you'd never want to even hang them up. Fuck my new life! It sounded terrible. I seriously questioned whether sobriety was for me. Maybe being unhealthy and making some piss-poor decisions was just the price I had to pay to keep having fun. It was surely better than making scarves and painting crappy artwork?

I promptly listened to a sober podcast to remind myself of the many reasons I had quit drinking. This was enough to put my head straight and at least think about what I could do to enjoy myself. I came to a quick realization that fun wasn't going to just come to me. I had to find fun – and it definitely wasn't going to be in the form of knitting my way to happiness. I didn't know what I liked or enjoyed because I had spent many years using wine as the remedy for boredom. The last time I remember having fun (sans wine) was when I was a teenager, before I started drinking at all. What did I enjoy doing then? Maybe that would be a good place to start? I loved music, particularly rock music. I started to learn to play the acoustic guitar when I was seven years old. I LOVED it. The school I went to offered free lessons. Unfortunately, when I was nine, my family relocated because my dad got a promotion. At that time, my parents couldn't afford for me to have private guitar lessons, and my new school didn't offer them, so I stopped playing. I suddenly realized that I could have taken up guitar any time since I'd been an adult. Why had I never thought of this? I still loved rock music. I still loved guitar. So, I bought one! I now take online lessons and self-teach on YouTube. Dare I say, I'm pretty good! Still a novice, granted. But I'm surprised at how much my hands still remembered from when I was a child. I picked it up quickly. I also booked concert tickets to see all the bands I love. I forgot just how exhilarating it is to be stood in among a crowd in a massive stadium, singing along to my favourite songs in unison with a bunch of strangers. A true "natural" high.

What else did I enjoy as a teenager? Roller coasters! Do I still enjoy those now? Absolutely! I promptly booked tickets to various theme parks. White-knuckle thrills are still something I love with a passion. I'd forgotten. Or more accurately, I just opted to do other activities that involved wine. Now I could explore other white-knuckle thrills. Maybe I could go bungee jumping? Or parasailing? The list is endless.

Finding ways to enjoy life and have fun while maintaining sobriety can be challenging. Many people are used to socializing or unwinding with alcohol, and it can be tough to imagine having fun without a drink in hand. However, there are many ways to enjoy life without relying on the poison, you just need to seek them out.

Stay active

As we've already covered, physical exercise is fantastic for your health, but it's a great way to have fun too! Not only can exercise help you feel better physically and emotionally, but it can also reduce stress and improve your overall health and levels of happiness. Even if you're as coordinated as a drunk penguin on ice, there's something out there for everyone. So, don't be afraid to try new things and get your sweat on. Who knows, maybe you'll discover a new passion for Zumba or pole dancing! Just remember to stretch before you unleash your inner Beyoncé.

Connect with others

Socializing is an essential part of having fun in sobriety. However, it's crucial to surround yourself with people who support your sobriety and won't pressure you to drink. When you're looking for friends to hang out with, make sure they're not just beer buddies, but buddies who don't mind sipping on a mocktail or two. Joining a support group can be a great way to find these people. You'll be able to share your journey with others who understand what you're going through and won't judge you for ordering water. If you're looking for a wild night out without the booze, attending sober events or parties is a great way to do it. There are plenty of options out there, from dance parties to mocktail-only events. I find it fun just looking for new events and experiences to try out. It's amazing how much you miss when your life revolves exclusively around a bar.

And finally, volunteering in your community is a fantastic way to meet like-minded people who share your values and goals. You'll get to make a difference in the world while making new friends – it's a win-win situation. Plus, if you volunteer at an animal shelter, you'll get to play with puppies, and who doesn't love that?

Plan outings and activities

Planning outings and activities can be an excellent way to have fun in sobriety. You can plan a weekend trip, a picnic or a visit to a local attraction. You can also plan a games night, a movie marathon or a cooking competition with friends or family. Having something to look forward to can provide a sense of excitement and anticipation, which can be a great source of fun and enjoyment. And let's not forget about the classic activity of karaoke! You can plan a group outing to a karaoke bar and sing your hearts out, even if you're not the next American idol. Remember, the point is to have fun and create memorable experiences with the people you care about, all while being completely sober!

Explore nature

Exploring nature is another great way to have fun in sobriety. You can go hiking, camping or fishing in the great outdoors. You can also visit local parks, gardens or nature reserves. Spending time in nature can be incredibly restful and rejuvenating. And if you're feeling really adventurous, you can even try to communicate with the animals using your best Tarzan voice. Just don't be surprised if all you get in return is a weird look from a passing bird. Exploring nature while sober is a great way to reconnect with the natural world and have some good old-fashioned fun. I was really surprised at how much I loved being outdoors when I became sober – I'd spent so much time hiding in my house when I was drinking, when I did get out, it was like discovering a whole new world. Sobriety can give you a real sense of adventure and zest for life. How will you spend yours?

Maintaining Freedom

"I'm very serious about no alcohol, no drugs.
Life is too beautiful."

Jim Carrey

Of all the clients I've worked with to help get sober, 100 per cent of them have at some point asked the question, "What do I do once this course has finished?" There is an understandable fear of going it alone, especially if you're using an accountability programme like mine, where you've had your hand held daily for three months. Once you're through the first 90 days of sobriety, your body returns to a state of "normal" and your brain and emotional state are stable, but the fear of relapse is terrifying for pretty much anyone with an addiction problem. I certainly felt this sense of dread in early sobriety. What if I just couldn't maintain it?

As I've already mentioned, I believe that this fear is perpetuated by the narrative communicated by 12-step programmes. Once you declare yourself an alcoholic, you're condemned to a life where relapse is always within spitting distance. You're never truly free. Sobriety is so fragile that it needs protecting like a newborn baby. As I've explained at length throughout this book, I fundamentally disagree with this point of view. You can completely recover, and if you fully buy into this outlook, maintaining sobriety isn't just possible, it's easy.

That said, there are countless ways to make life simpler and avoid triggers as much as possible. There are three particular things that are fundamental to ensuring I stay on the wagon: journalling, "quit lit" and making life as stress-free as possible. There is never a point in time where I don't have some form of addiction literature on the go. It's an easy way of ensuring that you continue to see no value in drinking alcohol and it stops you from developing a rose-tinted view with the passage of time. Journalling allows you to keep in check with your emotions, and it's so much easier to work out where you're going wrong when it's written down. By rating your levels of anxiety and depression out of ten each day, you can clearly see when things start to take a downward spiral. It allows you to catch problems early and solve them before they become overwhelming.

Lastly, I make my life as easy as I possibly can. When I was drinking, I had no idea how much I made my own life so extraordinarily difficult – not just because I was hanging out of my arse on a daily basis, but because I chose to navigate life without really giving much thought to the consequences of my decisions. I lived in chaos, so I spent most of my time firefighting and orbiting drama, rather than making life as easy and stress-free as it can be. Now I choose to constantly evaluate what I'm doing and why. I know that sounds quite exhausting, but it's actually quite fun to treat life like a series of escape rooms to circumnavigate. It's all just a game. And I really enjoy winning!

A huge amount of my daily existence centres around being a single mother. I'm actually pretty sure that God is a single mother. I think she spent six days running around sorting the whole fucking world out and then only got to rest on Sunday when the kids were shipped off to their dad's. That said, being a single mum does come with an awesome benefit: having every other weekend child-free. I always know I'm a stone's throw away from time to myself. I get an opportunity to reset and be totally selfish. But the upside of being a single mum is nothing compared to the benefits of being a sober one. Above all else, the ability to be present and make the most of the time I have with my boys is a huge reward in itself. I no longer second guess my parenting techniques because I trust my own judgement. I'm free to parent however I choose, even if it's entirely unconventional. I'd better give you some examples so you don't think I'm locking my kids in a dungeon and whipping them with belts for bad behaviour.

1 I treat parenting like I've got front-row seats at a real version of *The Hunger Games*

When my boys fight each other, I don't stress myself out by getting involved straightaway. If I try to interject, it doesn't stop: I tell them off, they wait until I'm finished, and then they hammer each other some more. By letting them go at it for a couple of rounds, the fights end much sooner. If one punches the other, they know damn well the retribution strike is coming, and it will escalate. It only took a couple of incidents before they started to realize that physical fighting is not the best idea. Since I've adopted this unconventional tactic, there has been a 90 per cent reduction in hitting. Obviously, I interject if it gets nasty – I'm not a monster (and I don't fancy mopping up blood) – but I think it's important for my boys to learn that in the real world, if you punch someone, they're probably going to punch you back. Best not to use your fists at all.

2 I let my boys swear in the house (minus the c-bomb)

Why? I was raised by a strict mother. All it made me want to do was rebel. I was never allowed to swear and now I have the mouth of a trucker. Strict rules were never going to work on me. By giving my boys a little rope and allowing them to be a bit naughty, I hoped it would make them less likely to go renegade, and they're going to learn swear words from friends at school in any event. It works a treat. They know that if they ever abuse the privilege and swear outside the house or in earshot of other people, they'll lose the concession. They've not broken this rule once. I recently went to my boys' school for parents' evening and their reports were so glowing it almost moved me to tears. One of the main things that stuck out was that both of their teachers said how impeccably mannered and kind they both are.

Who knows, I may change my mind if they go rogue on me, but for now, allowing a little bad behaviour seems to work. It also provides a lot of amusement. Every night when I put my boys to bed, we say three things that we're grateful for. On one occasion, Alfie said, "I'm grateful that I learned a new swear word today!"

"Oh really?! What is it then?" I replied.

"Not telling you," Alfie said with an ultra-cheeky grin on his face.

It seemed a little weird that he wouldn't tell me – given that he wouldn't get in trouble for saying it. After I said "Goodnight" and turned off the lights, Arthur said, "Night, Mum!" Alfie shouted, "Later, bitch!"

I howled with laughter. We all did. For ten straight minutes. His comedic timing was on point.

3   I lie – a lot

Now let me make this crystal clear, I do tell the honest truth for everything that matters, but lying is essential for me to get through each day unscathed and I'm a huge advocate of using it as a parenting tactic. For example, one morning, Alfie forgot his Roblox plush toy "Foxy", which he was excited to take to show-and-tell at school. Halfway to school, he realized he had forgotten it (despite 10,000 reminders) and asked me to turn the car around. I refused as it would have made us late. A shit show of a tantrum ensued. It astounds me how something as simple as a six-year-old forgetting a stuffed toy can result in a fit that would rival that of any toddler.

"You need to turn the car around now or I'm not going to school!" Alfie bawled.

"I can't, my darling. I'm really sorry, but you're going to have to ask the teacher if you can do show-and-tell tomorrow instead," I said with sympathetic tones.

"No! I'm not doing that! Get Foxy or I'm not getting out! You can't make me!"

"Okay, darling, that's fine. But we'll have to drive straight to jail I'm afraid. Mummy will be put in prison if I don't get you to school. It's the law. We'll have to find someone to look after you when we get there."

"Fine! I'll go! Aargh!" Excellent.

So, these are the types of lies I tell with enthusiastic exaggeration. I'm making the most of the time they're gullible. I won't be able to get away with this past the age of about 11, I reckon, so I better make the most of it now.

By no means am I recommending my parenting tactics as a solution to staying sober; however, any amount of stress reduction is worth it. We have curveballs constantly being thrown at us, so anything you can do to make the daily grind easier is worth doing, even if it is totally unconventional. There is no rule book on parenting, and there isn't a right or wrong way to raise *your* children. You're free to do whatever you damn well please. It's your life. It's so easy to lose sight of the fact that we only get one.

Whenever I'm having any sort of downward spiral, bad day or even a bad week, I always come back to one question:

Why the fuck are we here? Why are we wandering around on this planet, in this massive solar system? What's the point? I highly doubt that anyone will ever be able to answer this. And isn't that wonderful? We live in a world of infinite mystery. It's magical. In the absence of any evidence to the contrary, I choose to believe that life has one purpose – to enjoy it.

I feel best when I'm enjoying myself, so my life's mission is quite simple – to have as much fun as humanly possible. And yours can just as easily be too. Play jokes. Get laughs. Have adventures. Test your mettle. Dream big. Dream massive. Your new sober life is basically like becoming a kid again and seeing the world for the first time, through a new lens. A perfectly clear one. You get to feel every moment of gorgeous joy there is to experience. Sober, it's also much easier to minimize the bad stuff and keep it in perspective. Recover quickly. Move on. Find the joy again. Look at the world as one massive playground. It's waiting for you to explore. It's nothing short of a miracle that each and every one of us is here. We're so privileged to even get the chance to exist. And for that reason, after all the years of self-destruction, I'm not prepared to waste a minute of this extraordinary, beautiful life.

So, what are you waiting for? If you're toying with the idea of dipping your toes into sober water, you have nothing to lose and everything to gain. Just try 90 days and see how you feel. It will be the best decision you ever make for yourself. Only good things can come from it. Well, mostly.

I received a text message from one of the mums at school a few weeks ago, after her son came over for a playdate. This is what it said:

"Hi there, my son came home and told me that you have written a book and you're getting it published?! Well done you! I just wanted to quickly ask something as I was a bit concerned. He said Arthur told him that your book is about 'alcohol and vaginas'. I'm sure that he must have got this wrong but I thought I'd better check."

Mmm. Yeah, that's a great synopsis of this book, thanks Arthur.

Sober Mama Summary

1. *Stop drinking. Everything in life will get better.*
2. *If you have a Hagrid or a Gruffalo down there, it's probably best not to stand naked on a stage and show it to a club full of people.*

Epilogue

Dear Mum,

Today is the three-year anniversary of your death. It's hard to believe. So much has happened in the last three years, but it still feels like you were here just yesterday. I'm not sure it will ever truly sink in that you're gone and that I'll never get to talk to you again. There are so many things I want to say to you now, and many more things that I regret not having said when you were still with us. I hope that somewhere, you are still listening, because I'm finally ready to say them.

You always said the wrong thing at the wrong time. You had a knack for being insulting, in the most creative and bizarre of ways. You could never bring yourself to tell me that you were proud of me. You didn't show me much physical affection and I constantly felt like I was disappointing you. I tried so hard to impress you. The harder I tried, the less you praised me. I watched you love Steph in the way that I wanted to be loved. You seemed to love her effortlessly. When you died, this was all I could think about. I read your diary after your funeral. You'd made some comments about finding me difficult and that you were struggling to "get off my case". I was 11 years old at the time you wrote that entry. How was I so difficult to love at 11 years old? I was angry that you died. I wanted to yell at you. Scream at you. Ask you why you found me so fucking difficult to love. I spent the next two years trying to analyze this. I went to therapy. I told my therapist that I needed to work on processing my anger towards you and understand why you hated me. I discovered something I was not expecting.

I wanted to stay angry with you. I only ever focused on the negative. I didn't give you any credit for all the wonderful things that you did, because if I stayed angry with you, I'd never have to grieve. You may not have told me that you loved me very often, but you showed me it in countless other ways. When I was 11, you couldn't afford to buy me a top I desperately wanted for a school disco. I came home from school one day and you'd made it for me. You'd been to the local market and bought the material and a sewing pattern. You were busy on your sewing machine while I was at school. There was another time when I was going through my "goth" phase and I wanted my whole bedroom to be black. I came home one day and you'd made a duvet cover, pillowcase and curtains in black fabric. I was so delighted. You always put so much effort into buying and making gifts. I could mention something that I liked in passing, and you would always make a mental note. You were always listening. Every Christmas and birthday you would surprise me with something I had wanted, but not asked for. You may have struggled to praise me for my achievements, but if ever I was sad, you always went into instant maternal mode — that was when you always showed me affection.

Whenever I had a rough time, you were always the first person I wanted to call. You would always listen, and this was the time when you would always say the right things. When my sons were born, I watched as you showered them with love. At the time, it was hard, as I wished you had given that to me — but now I see that this was your way of showing me how much you did care. You loved my boys ferociously. You ran to my side when I was desperately sick after having Arthur. You flew back to the UK from Grand Cayman and on the day you landed, I begged you to come back and help because I was struggling so much with my health. You got on the next available flight. I lost count of the mornings you would gently knock on my bedroom door at five in the morning, when the boys were babies. The second you heard them stirring you would come into my bedroom and take them downstairs so I could get some much-needed rest and a lie in. If I ever needed help with babysitting, you'd always drop any other plans you had to be there. You constantly helped me around the house with cooking and laundry. I'd never ask. You just knew I needed help and did it anyway. You played with my boys constantly. Really played. They were too young to have electronic tablets at the time, but I know for certain that if you were still here, they would never have used them if you were around — because all they really ever want to do is to play, and you would have given every second of your time to them. The boys were so young when you died, but they remember you. They remember the attention you gave them. They miss you and they talk about you all the time.

I didn't want to think about how great you were. Because to acknowledge that is to accept that I've lost you. I'll never get to talk to you again. I'll never be able to hug you. I'll never be able to tell you the one thing that you desperately wanted to hear and that I never once said to you — you were a great mum. I will forever regret not saying that to you. I've finally been able to cry and grieve for your loss — for two reasons. Firstly, I've realized I was being a petulant child for only ever focusing on the negative. Secondly, I'm sober. For the first two years after you died, I drank more than I ever had. I was able to block out all of the emotions I didn't want to feel, by guzzling wine every single night. Your death was the catalyst for my drinking getting out of control and for me leaving my husband. My life became so dark. It's a horrible fact, because I would give anything to have you back, but your death is the reason I've been able to sort my life out. It's fucked up, painful and wonderful all at the same time.

Your death has shown me just how precious and fragile life is. I don't know how long I've got left on this planet and now I want to make every single day count. I wasted years in drunken oblivion. I'm not scared of dying anymore. I'm scared of not fulfilling my potential — a potential that would never have been possible without becoming sober. If you hadn't died, I'm not sure I would ever have found the strength to stop drinking. I wouldn't have gone to therapy. I wouldn't have turned my life around. Your death has given me my purpose in life — to help other people get sober and turn their lives around too. I never felt like I had a purpose before. A reason for living. This is the biggest gift I could have ever received. I spent a lifetime trying to get your approval when what I really needed to do was approve of myself. I didn't like who I was. I didn't love myself. Now I do. I've realized that many of my qualities have come from you, and more importantly, all the things I perceived as negative have taught me the most amazing lessons. I wouldn't be the woman I am now if you weren't the mum that you were for me.

I have always strived to be the best I can be. If I hadn't been so desperate for your approval, I would never have grown to be so ambitious. I lavish my boys with physical and verbal affection, because this was something I wanted from you more than anything. You taught me how important this is. This isn't a criticism in any way. You had an extraordinarily tough upbringing and you didn't have a role model for how to be a mum. You had no love or affection from your mother and you had to deal with some truly awful realities while growing up. You may not have been able to show physical love and affection the way I wanted, but you did show me that you loved me in countless other ways. I just didn't want to acknowledge them at the time. I was too selfish to see it.

I am so grateful that you were my mum. If all the mums were lined up around the world and I had to choose one, I would have chosen you. You were wonderful. I am so sorry I never told you. I hope you can hear me. I hope you can see the person I am now. I hope you are proud. I promise not to waste a single day of my beautiful life. The life that you gave to me. I'll see you on the other side. I'll love you always.

My 90-Day Freedom Programme

As a result of my personal experience, I have developed a 90-day programme specifically designed for mums who want to quit drinking. This programme consists of seven practical modules that are delivered through a hybrid course (part online and part in person on Zoom), daily accountability emails and Zoom meetings. Each module is designed to address a different aspect of the recovery process, providing women with the tools and resources they need to overcome their addiction and live a sober life.

I turned my recovery method into a programme because I found a formula that works and I feel very strongly that my purpose in life is to help other mums get sober. The years of fuck-ups, bad decisions and huge mistakes I've made in this life were so I could get to this place. The place in my life where I can make up for my many failings, and help other people. I'm not so deluded as to think that I've found the ultimate winning formula that will work for everyone. I don't think there will ever be a single programme that can do that. But for those women who have been a good fit for my process and enrolled in my programme, I have been very successful in helping them to achieve sobriety.

I help mums identify the underlying causes of their addiction and develop effective coping mechanisms to deal with triggers and cravings. I also provide guidance on building a support network and establishing healthy habits to support their recovery journey.

I understand that quitting drinking is not an easy feat, especially for mums who have many responsibilities and commitments. That's why my programme is designed to be simple, flexible and adaptable to each woman's unique situation. Whether you're a stay-at-home mum or working, whether you have a supportive partner or not, my programme is tailored to meet your individual needs.

I have seen incredible success stories from women who have completed my 90-day programme and been able to maintain their sobriety and go on to live fulfilling, happy lives. My greatest joy comes from seeing these women transform and achieve their goals. You can find success stories on my website and the Facebook group below.

If you're a mum struggling with alcohol addiction, I encourage you to take the first step towards recovery by having a chat with me to identify your three biggest blockers to becoming sober. You don't have to face this journey alone. With my support and guidance, you can overcome your addiction and live a healthy, happy and sober life.

NB: This programme is not a substitute for therapy/counselling. If you are engaging with a therapist, then I recommend you continue with this throughout the course.

www.sobermama.co.uk
My blog: www.whymummygaveupdrinking.co.uk
Instagram: instagram.com/sobermamaltd
YouTube: youtube.com/@SoberMamaLtd
Spotify: podcasters.spotify.com/pod/show/rachael-shephard

You can access my Sober Mama Facebook page using the below QR code. From there, you can access my "Sober Mama" Facebook group in the About section. This is a wonderful, supportive group of women who are trying to get sober – or who have achieved sobriety and want to help others in the group with their struggles.

Contact: info@sobermama.co.uk

Acknowledgements

To Sophie (my beautiful editor) and Summersdale Publishers (Hachette UK). Thank you so much for taking a chance on me as a new author. To this day, I still can't believe this book is actually being published and I'm eternally grateful that you gave me this opportunity.

To my dearest of friends, Kelly, Em, Becca, Gem, Sam, Pete and Cheryl – I love you guys so much. Thank you for listening to me endlessly bang on about the content of this book and for giving me your suggestions. I'd be lost without each of you and I'm unbelievably grateful to have you all in my life.

To Sara, my darling friend. You will never leave my thoughts and you'll be in my heart always. I'm blessed to have known you and I am so excited to see your beautiful daughter grow into her own woman – and in the shape of her most incredible mother.

To my darling sister, Steph, I love you with all my heart. Thank you for your endless support, love and kindness. I'm so excited for all the memories we've yet to make and all the fun times to come. Mum would be so proud of everything you're doing with your life. As am I. You're so loved by me and the boys.

My dear darling dad. It's hard to find the words to express my gratitude. You've always been my number one believer and supporter. You're the first person I want to call whenever anything goes wrong or right. I could not have wished for a better dad. You're always there, whenever I need you. You gave me the belief that I could achieve anything I put my mind to. This book wouldn't exist without you. I'm so proud of how you've come through the past four years. From the bottom of my heart, thank you for being my dad. You're the best.

To my beautiful, gorgeous boys, Arthur and Alfie. My world. I could write a whole other book just on the ways you make me happy. You're both still so young and I'm already so immensely proud of the wonderful little men you're becoming. You're the kindest, sweetest, funniest souls and I'm eternally grateful for the endless cuddles and affirmations of love you both give. I'm the luckiest mama on the planet.

And to my beautiful mum. Thank you for being the mother you were and for inspiring me to be the best mum that I can be. I wouldn't be who I am without you. I'll miss you always. Until we meet again.

Sources

Introduction – Why I Quit Alcohol for Good

Page 11 – "The reality is that we regularly consume one of the most addictive and damaging drugs…"

americanaddictioncenters.org/adult-addiction-treatment-programs/most-addictive

Page 12 – "Here's a fun fact: just 80 to 90 millilitres of pure ethanol can kill you…"

empendium.com/mcmtextbook/chapter/B31.II.20.2.1.

Page 12 – "Yet, booze is the single biggest killer of working-age adults…"

www.rehab4addiction.co.uk/blog/alcohol-misuse-biggest-cause-working-age-mortality-england

Page 12–13 – "I read one article which suggested that red wine lowers heart disease…"
www.mayoclinic.org/diseases-conditions/heart-disease/in-depth/red-wine/art-20048281

Page 15 – "Alcohol doesn't help you to relax…"
www.drinkaware.co.uk/facts/health-effects-of-alcohol/mental-health/alcohol-and-stress

Page 17 – "Shockingly, at the top of the list are some of the most highly paid (and stressful) careers…"

choicespsychotherapy.net/jobs-with-highest-suicide-rates/

Page 17 – "'Year after year, both dentist and doctor remain… highest suicide rates…'"

www.mentalhealthdaily.com

Page 17 – "Doctors in particular are well known for being prone to developing alcohol and drug addictions…"

www.ncbi.nlm.nih.gov/pmc/articles/PMC2704134/

www.rcpsych.ac.uk/docs/default-source/members/
supporting-you/pss/pss-14-drug-and-alcohol-problems.
pdf?sfvrsn=7eba96_2

Moderate, or Quit for Good?

Page 22 – "Because Mother Nature very cleverly equipped your tongue with tastebuds – so you have the ability to assess what you ingest, to make sure it's safe…"

pubmed.ncbi.nlm.nih.gov/16983846/

Am I an Alcoholic?

Page 33 – "In the Oxford English Dictionary, an alcoholic is defined as 'a person who regularly drinks too much alcohol…'"

www.oxfordlearnersdictionaries.com/definition/english/
alcoholic_2

Page 34 – "The World Health Organization recently published a statement… there is no safe amount that does not affect health…"

www.who.int/europe/news/item/04-01-2023-no-level-of-alcohol-consumption-is-safe-for-our-health

Page 35 – "According to Wikipedia, a high-functioning alcoholic is a 'person who maintains jobs and relationships while exhibiting alcoholism'…"

en.wikipedia.org/wiki/High-functioning_alcoholic

Page 37 – "Drinking makes your skin look sallow, causes premature ageing, weight gain, acne and weakens your hair and nails…"

www.healthline.com/health/alcohol-and-hair-loss

Page 37 – "Drinking actually shrinks the size of your brain…"

drinkwise.org.au/under-18s/how-alcohol-affects-your-brain/

Page 37 – "Alcohol causes multiple types of cancer and liver cirrhosis…"

www.cancerresearchuk.org/about-cancer/liver-cancer/risks-causes

Page 37 – "Alcohol causes depression…"

www.mentalhealth.org.uk/explore-mental-health/a-z-topics/alcohol-and-mental-health

Page 37 – "Alcohol significantly increases domestic violence in seriousness and frequency…"
alcoholchange.org.uk/alcohol-facts/fact-sheets/alcohol-and-domestic-abuse

Alcohol Causes Fun and Excitement, Right?

Page 54 – "The prefrontal cortex of your brain, which is responsible for rational thinking and decision-making, becomes flawed when it has been lubricated by alcohol…"
livefreerecoverynh.com/how-do-drugs-and-alcohol-affect-decision-making/

Page 57 – "When we have our first drink, the brain releases dopamine…."
www.mariongluckclinic.com/blog/how-does-alcohol-affect-your-hormones.html
www.ncbi.nlm.nih.gov/pmc/articles/PMC6826820/
www.drugrehab.com/addiction/alcohol/alcoholism/alcohol-and-dopamine/

Page 57 – "It only takes ten minutes for alcohol to kick in…"
www.healthline.com/health/how-long-does-it-take-for-alcohol-to-kick-in

Page 57 – "The body reacts to the presence of alcohol and needs to achieve homeostasis – balance…"
www.verywellmind.com/the-link-between-stress-and-alcohol-67239

Page 57 – "The brain recognizes that it has unusually high levels of dopamine, so it seeks to bring those back into balance by releasing cortisol – the stress hormone…"

www.ncbi.nlm.nih.gov/pmc/articles/PMC2266962/

www.verywellmind.com/heavy-drinking-increases-stress-hormone-63201

Page 58 – "When we quit drinking, it takes up to 90 days of sobriety for the brain to start firing up and producing dopamine on its own again…"

hickorytreatmentcenters.com/2022/09/how-long-does-it-take-for-dopamine-to-reset/

The Four Stages of Alcoholism

Page 69–70 – "The liver has no nerve endings, so it can't tell you when it's fucked…"

www.mountelizabeth.com.sg/health-plus/article/signs-of-a-failing-liver

Page 72 – "Elvin Morton Jellinek was a scientist who specialized in alcohol addiction research…"

sober.com/addictions/stages-of-alcoholism/

alcohol.org/alcoholism-types/stages/

What Happens When You Stop Drinking – the Timeline

Page 79 – "Even if we plan to have only one drink, the prefrontal cortex (the decision-making part of our brain) starts to change…"

www.ncbi.nlm.nih.gov/pmc/articles/PMC4523220/

Page 82 – "Alcohol withdrawal usually lasts between three and seven days from the time of your last drink – but can be a little longer…"

www.nhs.uk/conditions/alcohol-misuse/treatment/

Page 84 – "Withdrawal symptoms end, just like that. Ten short days in…"

www.therecoveryvillage.com/alcohol-abuse/withdrawal-detox/

www.verywellmind.com/is-this-normal-how-long-will-it-last-80197

Page 85 – "When you consume ethanol, you lose approximately four times as much liquid as you actually consumed – because it's a diuretic…"

www.ardurecoverycenter.com/alcohol-effects-on-hydration/

Page 86 – "'I can feel my brain shrinking' after a heavy night. Little did I know that it actually was…"

www.alzheimers.org.uk/about-dementia/types-dementia/alcohol-related-brain-damage-arbd

Page 86 – "Alcohol is a pretty nasty irritant and damages the stomach lining…"

www.drinkaware.co.uk/facts/health-effects-of-alcohol/general-health-effects/is-alcohol-harming-your-stomach

Page 88–89 – "Common feelings and experiences include…"

www.healthline.com/health/pink-cloud#tips

Page 89 – "So why does pink cloud happen? Some researchers believe it occurs because the body comes out of a state of withdrawal, and it's a symptom of relief now that the body is starting to heal…"

www.forbes.com/health/conditions/pink-cloud/

Page 92 – "An alcohol-free sleep cycle has four different stages: three non-rapid eye movement (NREM) stages and one REM stage…"

courses.lumenlearning.com/waymaker-psychology/chapter/stages-of-sleep/

Page 93 – "Alcohol is a sedative, making it easy to fall into a deep sleep quickly…"

www.sleepfoundation.org/nutrition/alcohol-and-sleep

Page 96 – "After three weeks of not drinking, your blood pressure will begin to decrease…"

www.priorygroup.com/blog/benefits-of-giving-up-alcohol-for-a-month

Page 96 – "Alcohol increases blood levels of the hormone renin, which causes the blood vessels to get smaller in diameter, putting increased pressure on the vessel walls and causing hypertension…"

www.medicalnewstoday.com/articles/alcohol-and-blood-pressure

Page 96 – "In week four, removing alcohol from your body will improve your liver function…"

columbiasurgery.org/liver/liver-and-its-functions

mydr.com.au/gastrointestinal-health/liver-and-alcohol-breakdown/

Page 97 – "Alcohol has been shown to negatively affect the proper functioning of the hippocampus, the area of your brain that deals with memory…"

sites.duke.edu/apep/module-3-alcohol-cell-suicide-and-the-adolescent-brain/content/alcohol-memory-and-the-hippocampus/

Harm Reduction – and the Dangers of Switching One Addiction for Another

Page 148 – "How long does it take nicotine to leave the human body? You're 97 per cent nicotine-free after just six hours. After 48 hours, you're entirely nicotine-free…"

www.allencarr.com/easyway-stop-smoking/nicotine-withdrawal-timeline/

Getting High

Page 156 – "While I've never taken heroin, I can imagine how it feels, having once been prescribed 'hillbilly heroin' – oxycodone…"

truhealinggaithersburg.com/blog/oxycodone-vs-heroin-is-one-safer/

Alcohol and Anxiety

Page 170 – "Now consider that the human mind has between 12 thousand and 60 thousand thoughts a day…"

tlexinstitute.com/how-to-effortlessly-have-more-positive-thoughts/

Why Is it so Hard to Find Out How to Quit?

Page 207 – "AA was founded by Bill Wilson in 1935…"

en.wikipedia.org/wiki/Alcoholics_Anonymous

Lance Dodes and Zachary Dodes, *The Sober Truth: Debunking the Bad Science Behind 12-Step Programs and the Rehab Industry* (2015)

www.castlecraig.co.uk/addiction-resources/the-sober-truth-a-new-book-that-disputes-aas-effectiveness/

Have you enjoyed this book?

If so, why not write a review on your favourite website?

If you're interested in finding out more about our books,
find us on Facebook at **Summersdale Publishers**,
on Twitter/X at **@Summersdale** and on Instagram and
TikTok at **@summersdalebooks** and get in touch.
We'd love to hear from you!

Thanks very much for buying this Summersdale book.

www.summersdale.com